The
HEPTARCHIA
MYSTICA

The HEPTARCHIA MYSTICA
of
John Dee

Thoth Publications

Portrait of John Dee (c. 1594) Artist Unknown, Ashmolean Museum, Oxford.

The HEPTARCHIA MYSTICA of John Dee

Transcribed, Introduced and Annotated by
Robert Turner
Foreword by Anne Turner

Third Edition revised and edited
with contributory articles by
Robin E. Cousins

Latin translations by
Christopher Upton

Illustrated by
Charles H. Cattell

First published in a limited edition by
Magnum Opus Hermetic Sourceworks, Edinburgh, 1983.

Second enlarged edition published by The Aquarian Press,
Wellingborough, Northamptonshire, 1986.

Preface, Historical Foreword, Introduction, Transcription,
Appendices A, B, D
© The Estate of Robert Turner, 2023

Foreword © Anne Turner, 2023

Preface to Third Edition, Appendices C and E
© Robin E. Cousins, 2023

Latin Translations © The Estate of Christopher Upton, 2023

Illustrations © Charles H. Cattell, 2023

Ministers for the Days of the Week © Dave Marsh, 2023

This edition published by Thoth Publications 2023

Robert Turner and Robin Cousins asserts the moral right to be
identified as the authors of this work.

A CIP catalogue record for this book is available from
the British Library

All rights reserved. No part of this publication may be
reproduced, stored in a retrieval system, or transmitted,
in any form or by any means, electronic, mechanical,
photocopying, recording or otherwise, without the
prior permission of the publishers.

Cover and text design by Helen Surman

Published by Thoth Publications
2 Copt Oak Cottage, Whitwick Road, Markfield,
Leicestershire LE67 9QB
Web address: www.thoth.co.uk   email: enquiries@thoth.co.uk

DEDICATION by Robert Turner

*To the memory of my good friend
the late Gerald Yorke,
who did so much to aid the development of
the Western Magical Tradition.*

CONTENTS

FOREWORD by Anne Turner	13
PREFACE to the Third Edition	19
ROBERT TURNER'S ACKNOWLEDGEMENTS for the Second Edition	21
PREFACE to the Second Edition	23
Historical Foreword	25
INTRODUCTION	31
DE HEPTARCHIA MYSTICA	47
APPENDIX A: Analytical Notes	107
APPENDIX B: John Dee's Religious Magic	137
APPENDIX C: Mortlake Revisted by Robin E. Cousins	147
APPENDIX D: The Voynich Manuscript and an Ancient Treasure Map	163
APPENDIX E: The Heptarchical Angelic Hierarchy: an Overview by Robin E. Cousins	173
Select Bibliography	185

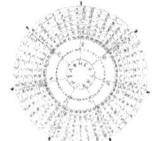

FOREWORD by Anne Turner
Thank you for making me curious.

AS with most pieces of writing it is difficult to know where to start. I am not a writer, but the daughter of two brilliantly talented parents who wrote about the most interesting things. So, I took a leaf out of my Mum's book and started to research! First I noted down all my memories that were linked to the writing and publishing of *The Heptarchia Mystica of John Dee*. Then I re-read the appendices in the book writing down things that struck a chord with me; and finally to complete my secondary research, I revisited some paperwork that I recently found in the form of a very useful bio that Dad wrote in c. 1985. And there you have it, the basis for my foreword to Dad's prized work – I hope I can do him proud.

When I was in my early teens, Dad was completing his research and writing his manuscript for the second edition of the *Heptarchia* – he was very excited. The work of John Dee was his passion and he was really proud that his work was going to be published again so quickly (the limited edition first edition came out in 1983). This is especially poignant as he left school with one O level in Physics having being told by

THE HEPTARCHIA MYSTICA

the teachers that he would never amount to anything. How wrong could they be? This volume proves both his academic and scholarly worth.

Growing up, Dad had a home environment where matters beyond the normal scope of religious education were discussed freely; this sparked his initial interest in occultism. This echoes my own childhood where I was surrounded by books of every kind and the pictures of John Dee and his contemporaries that adorned Dad's study wall – Dr Dee was very familiar to me, those eyes watched over me as I poured though books on the Qabalah, feeding my latest fascination with the Ark of the Covenant. At 11 years old I could not have realised that Dad was going to write in his commentary how Dee's Holy Table took on a semblance of the Hebrew Ark of the Covenant with its silken trappings and insulation from the earth.

Whilst still in his teens, Dad had a chance encounter with a man who he describes in his bio as, "*…an elderly, sage-like personality*" who "*…produced a tremendous and lasting impact on my life.*" This 'Master' fed him information on Alchemy, the Qabalah, Ceremonial Magic and (most importantly), the seed idea of John Dee's Enochian System all in bite-sized, digestible chunks. This all fascinated him a great deal, but his fascination crystallised on the strange Angelic Invocations penned by Dr John Dee in Elizabethan England.

A couple of years later, Dad received an invitation to visit Gerald Yorke (the late Squire of Forthampton and distinguished associate of Aleister Crowley). His subsequent friendship with Yorke gave him the confidence to continue his quest into researching Dee. Dad writes, "*From the outset, he encouraged my researches, recounting tales of Crowley's adventures*

FOREWORD

in Dee's universe…and allowing me to examine and even take away little known and unpublished manuscripts; while introducing me to a whole host of magical authorities…" Dad's gratitude to Gerald Yorke is echoed in his dedication of this work to his memory.

Skip forward nearly two decades incorporating extensive research (including close examination and translation of original manuscripts in the British Library), lecturing prolifically on magic in the Tudor period and additional in-depth research by his colleagues in the Order of the Cubic Stone; he was ready for publication.

We cannot forget Mum's involvement in all this. Always in the background, her capacity as a walking dictionary as well as being an authority on historical matters, ritual magic and magical alphabets was invaluable to Dad whilst he was researching and writing the *Heptarchia*.

When the second edition was published in 1986, there were a few aspects that I was absolutely obsessed with. There were a lot of 'B's, there was a drawing of a 'devilish face' that if you turned it upside down it was a man with a beard and my greatest source of fascination being the section on the Voynich Manuscript and the Ancient Treasure Map. I was also extremely proud of my Dad that he had published his book and that he was featured in local papers and radio stations recognising his achievements.

I now know that the 'B's represent the 49 Good Angels. That the Voynich Manuscript is most probably an alchemical document by Francis Bacon (13th Century Friar) and could have been sold by Dee to Rudolph II for 600 golden ducats! The Ancient Treasure Map then, as it does now, still looks like a collection of crosses, ink-wells, feathers and a litter bin. But

THE HEPTARCHIA MYSTICA

I now understand that it was found by Edward Kelley (Dee's conjurer) in 1582 and shows a table of locations and objects leading to the hidden treasure of Menabani of Gordania; with said 'litter bin' more than likely being a bee hive. I suppose, as a young teenager, and as someone looking from the inside out, I saw things very differently.

My humble opinion today is that John Dee is for everyone's consumption. In fact, over the centuries he has grown from a mysterious figure to being embedded in popular culture. Shakespeare started it with the character of Prospero in *The Tempest*. In the late 1980s, there was a theatre production called the *Queen's Magus* that peeled back the veil a little further. 2007 saw *Elizabeth: The Golden Age* (starring Cate Blanchett) acknowledge the importance of his role as Elizabeth I's astrologer and, continuing to the present day, where John Dee, Edward Kelley and Dee's Library all feature in Deborah Harkness's "*A Discovery of Witches*" (2018-22). Imagine my glee and excitement when I binge watched the first two seasons and wondered what Dad would have thought? He probably would have moaned about the inaccuracies, but would have been secretly proud that Dee had made his way all the way from the Elizabethan era to the present day and be a recognised figure to the general populous.

The meticulous nature of both my late parents led to this book been written and published. An unfortunate set of circumstances prevented it from being republished sooner. Dad was a worthy contributor to occult lore and tradition and his works and achievements should be made accessible to future generations. I am therefore greatly indebted to Robin E Cousins and Thoth Publications for helping ensure this knowledge is passed on.

FOREWORD

And so, in dedication to my Dad – the writer, electrician, sword fencer, keen gardener and local eccentric and my Mum – the book worm, writer, prolific researcher, chutney maker and academic; we secure this legacy.

In the words of the Egyptians,
"*...to speak the name of the dead is to make them live again.*"
In loving memory of Robert Turner (1944-2013) and Patricia Shore Turner (1945-2020).

Anne Turner,
Wolverhampton, March 2023

PREFACE
to the Third Edition
Dedicated to Robert and Patricia Turner

FORTY years have passed since Robert Turner first published John Dee's *Heptarchia Mystica* in 1983. It proved so popular that a second revised and enlarged edition quickly followed in 1986. Having been long out-of-print, a new edition is well overdue. Regrettably, Robert Turner died in 2013 and with the passing of his wife Patricia in 2020, it was felt that a new third edition of the *Heptarchia* would be an appropriate tribute to them.

Several years ago, Robert had in fact asked me to help prepare a new edition of the *Heptarchia* for publication, but unfortunately it never materialised. However, after recent discussions with Robert and Patricia's daughter, Anne Turner, we decided to resurrect the project and this new edition is the result. Anne has kindly written a delightful Foreword commemorating her parents and their legacy to Enochian magic and the Western Magical Tradition via the mystery school centred within the legendary Order of the Cubic Stone.

This memorial edition has been completely revised and

THE HEPTARCHIA MYSTICA

updated. Special thanks are due to Alan Thorogood for providing additional historical information, which has been incorporated into the text; to Charles H. Cattell, once again, for his illustrations; to Barbara Prichard for a new translation of Edward Kelley's treasure map text; to Dave Marsh for compiling the table: *Ministers for the Days of the Week*; and, finally, to the late Christopher Upton for his Latin translations.

Dr Upton passed away in 2015. He was a prominent Birmingham historian, university lecturer and a regular columnist for the *Birmingham Post*. He also worked as a historical consultant for the BBC TV programme *Peaky Blinders*.

Contributors to various footnotes and additional text are identified by their initials in square brackets, namely: RT – Robert Turner, AT – Alan Thorogood, and REC – Robin E. Cousins. Additional text in the main body is followed by the initials of the contributor and the whole is contained within square brackets.

The illustrations have been digitally remastered for this new edition which also benefits from additional photographs and other artwork. All sources are gratefully acknowledged. Some items are in the public domain and if this was indeterminable, every reasonable effort has been made to locate the copyright holders.

Finally, I should like to express my gratitude to Tom Clarke and Thoth Publications for their help and enthusiasm in making this new edition of the *Heptarchia* a reality.

Robin E. Cousins
Norwich, March 2023

Robert Turner's
ACKNOWLEDGEMENTS
for the Second Edition

DURING the course of preparing this book for publication I have incurred the debt of many friends, colleagues and public institutions, without whose help the work could not have been completed.

My grateful thanks are due to the British Library for its permission to reproduce the first folio of John Dee's *De Heptarchia Mystica* (Sloane MS 3191) and Edward Kelley's treasure map (Sloane MS 3188); to the late Desmond Bourke and the staff of the British Library's Department of Manuscripts for their tireless assistance throughout the duration of my studies; and to the Beinecke Rare Book and Manuscript Library of Yale University, Connecticut, for permission to publish a page from the Voynich manuscript.

I am greatly indebted to my old friend Charles Cattell for his talented and enthusiastic rendering of the *Heptarchia's* complex and daunting artwork, to Robin Cousins for his contribution on ancient Mortlake and to Christopher Upton for his translation of Dee's Latin.

THE HEPTARCHIA MYSTICA

My thanks also to the late Theodore Howard, William Cammies, Stephen Lauder, Christian Wilby, and to the staff of Wolverhampton Public Libraries, all of whom came forward with constructive help and encouragement during the various stages of my work.

Special thanks to my wife Patricia for information regarding historical matters; for her many valuable suggestions, and for undertaking the unenviable task of proof-reading the entire text.

Finally, I wish to offer my sincerest gratitude to my publishers whose capable, friendly, and active participation has made this new edition of the *Heptarchia* possible.

PREFACE
to the Second Edition

SINCE the first appearance of this work[1], so much has transpired, on so many levels, that it has become necessary to present this amended and expanded version of John Dee's *De Heptarchia Mystica* to the public.

In this new rendering we have been at pains to make good the various shortcomings of the preliminary transcription by careful re-examination of Dee's original manuscript. Errors arising from initial difficulties in interpreting the Elizabethan hand have now, it is hoped, been eradicated, resulting in a more intelligible and coherent text. Additionally, I have been fortunate enough to find Dr Christopher Upton, an apt and erudite scholar who has dealt admirably with the Latin elements in the work. His translations of the integrated section headings and sub-notes greatly enhance the value of the book, making hitherto opaque aspects of Dee's treatise available to the non-Latin reader.

To emphasize John Dee's involvement with cryptology and antiquarian matters, I have appended an entirely new item

1. *The Heptarchia Mystica of John Dee*, Edinburgh: Magnum Opus Hermetic Sourceworks, 1983.

THE HEPTARCHIA MYSTICA

regarding the enigmatic Voynich Manuscript, and a curious Treasure map which came into Dee's possession while engaged in his early Angelic experiments. It is hoped that these and other inclusions will prove of interest to both occultist and historian.

The exact location of John Dee's Mortlake home is to this day a subject of some speculation, and due to the state of abject poverty in which Dee lived out the final years of his life, only the faintest details of his burial at the Church of St Mary continue to survive. In order to place the various interrelated aspects of this book in proper context and to paint as accurate a picture as possible of John Dee's life and times, I felt it necessary to furnish the reader with any information which could be obtained regarding these long-neglected matters.

On the subject of Elizabethan and modern Mortlake I therefore consulted Robin Cousins, a young colleague who has conducted extensive antiquarian researches in the Richmond upon Thames area. Robin agreed to investigate historic Mortlake with particular reference to John Dee and to add his findings as a concluding section to this volume.

In *Mortlake Revisited*, Robin Cousins reveals many fascinating and little-known details regarding Dee's home town, the position of the old house (now long demolished), and provides us with a description of the 'good Doctor's' last resting place which powerfully evokes the wretched circumstances that finally engulfed Elizabethan England's greatest magus.

Robert Turner
February 1985

HISTORICAL FOREWORD

THE richness of the Elizabethan epoch — perhaps the greatest period in British history — can be seen as the reflection of those great minds which interwove to produce the glittering tapestry of their time. In this age of worthies, there arose a man of great talents: John Dee. Mathematician, astronomer, geographer and historian, he was a man of great genius whose merits were extolled by royalty and nobility alike; a true Renaissance scholar, equal in every way to the finest minds of his era.

Dee's erudition endeared him to Queen Elizabeth I, who appointed him as her Astrologer Royal and counsellor on certain matters of state and scientific importance. Yet, in spite of his prominence in the Elizabethan world, Dee remains strangely neglected by latter day historians. It is scarcely necessary to furnish the reader with a detailed account of John Dee's life, as the subject has been adequately dealt with elsewhere.[2] A single quotation — if rather turgid and pontifical — from Dr Thomas Smith's *The Life of John Dee* will suffice to indicate the course of Dee's earlier life and development:

---

2. Peter French. *John Dee: the World of an Elizabethan Magus* . London: Routledge and Kegan Paul, 1972.

THE HEPTARCHIA MYSTICA

John Dee first drew the breath of life at London on the 13th day of the month of July, at 4 o'clock and 11 minutes p.m. in the year of the eternal incarnated Word 1527. His father was Roland Dee, an honourable man, and coming of a family sufficiently genteel, whose care, according to the affection implanted by nature towards his own son, as well as his being a boy of great hope and good disposition, was chiefly bestowed in informing his mind with Greek and Latin literature. The curriculum of the studies in which boys are accustomed to be taught being happily passed, partly in London, partly in Chelmsford in the County of Essex, he was entered by his most loving father in the 16th year of his age, at Cambridge, in the College dedicated to the memory of St John the Evangelist, to be taught the higher Sciences, at the end of the year 1542.[3]

At Cambridge Dee devoured knowledge at an incredible rate, working at his books and tutorials for up to eighteen hours a day. In 1548 he attained to the degree of Master of Arts and left Cambridge to further his education on the continent. His fame spread throughout Europe, and in his twenty-third year (1550) he lectured on Euclid to enthusiastic audiences at the University of Paris.

It seems that Dee's reputation as a philosopher stood him in good stead with the English court throughout two reigns, marred only by his brief imprisonment – falsely accused of conjuring spirits – under Mary, in June 1555. Some measure of Elizabeth's esteem for her philosopher can be gleaned from the fact that in 1558 Dee was appointed to erect a horoscope in order to ascertain the most favourable date for her coronation.

Dee was a prolific writer, producing innumerable books

---

3. Thomas Smith. *The Life of John Dee, an English Mathematician*, translated from the Latin by Wm. Alexr. Ayton. The Theosophical Publishing Society, London, 1908. First published as *Vita Joannis Dee* in 1707.

HISTORICAL FOREWORD

and manuscripts throughout his long life span. These works covered a vast and varied range of subjects: the arts, sciences and philosophies were all represented in admirable and studious detail, some being so long and complex that printers refused to accept them. In 1570, Dee published his widely acclaimed *Mathematicall Preface* to the English edition of Euclid's *Geometry* (*The Elements of Geometrie of the most auncient Philosopher Euclide of Megara*, trans. Sir Henry Billingsley, London, 1570), a work of great originality and erudition which exerted a powerful influence on sixteenth century scientific thought.

Few of Dee's works have been reprinted in modern times, the one notable exception being *The Hieroglyphic Monad,* which since its first appearance in Antwerp in 1564 has passed through six editions and is still available to this day. In this work, Dee attempts to symbolize the homogeneity of the Universe and the Creator, each individual element being portrayed as an interrelating component of the Monad, represented as a Mercuric emblem combined with the point and binary crescents.

Aside from his personal literary pursuits Dee was a prodigious collector of books. His library amounted to some three thousand volumes and several hundred manuscripts, rivalling any collection in the Elizabethan world. These, together with a vast array of Celtic records, ancient seals and genealogies, were preserved at his house in Mortlake.

Dee's Mortlake home also housed his collection of scientific instruments. Astrolabes, quadrants, globes, all manner of optical and navigational equipment filled his laboratories. In his *The Life of John Dee*, Thomas Smith describes the contents of Dee's library as follows:

THE HEPTARCHIA MYSTICA

To the noble furniture of the Library, there appertained a not moderate accumulation of Mathematical Instruments and Machines: also those which at that time had not been brought into common use, as well as those which by his own ingenuity amended and reformed he had brought into a better condition, amongst which that I may omit the rest, were a quadrant and a staff, the semi-diameter of it being five feet, but of this, ten, accurately marked with divisions, the globe of Mercator, amended and improved by the help of new observations, by means of which he had inserted the places and motions of the Comets, which appeared at their proper time, the octave, the ninth and tenth of their spheres, according to the hypothesis of the theory of Purbachius, ornamented with a horizon and brass meridian; mariner's compasses of various kinds and fabricated to find the variation; and lastly, a clock, which, in that age, was held almost for a miracle, adapted to measure the second minutes of the hour...

Dee invented various navigational instruments of his own design, amongst them a device which he called the Paradoxical Compass, which could be corrected to avoid charting errors. Mariners, however, mistrusted this new innovation (or, more likely, could not understand the complex principle of its operation), and it was rarely used.

Strangely enough, it was Dee's inventive talents that first gave rise to his reputation as a sorcerer. In his early Cambridge days he was responsible for a production of Aristophanes' *Pax*, for which he contrived a mechanical beetle or Scarabeus, to fly through the air to the Palace of Jupiter, carrying a man and a basket of food. This feat so astonished the audience, who were for the most part ignorant of the mechanical arts, that rumours were spread to the effect that Dee had accomplished

HISTORICAL FOREWORD

this wonder by the aid of demons. Similar superstitious beliefs followed him wherever he went, even during the time he and his family were journeying on the continent in the 1580s.

Dee spent most of his life in a state of penury, the majority of his meagre income being taken up in the care of his family and his insatiable appetite for books and travel, for although Queen Elizabeth from time to time sent him gifts of money, it was not until 1596 that she granted him a living as Warden of Christ's College, Manchester.

After the death of Elizabeth in 1603, Dee's life and health drastically deteriorated. His reputation as a magician continued to hamper him and even in Manchester, he encountered hostility. The Queen's successor James I, author of *Demonology* – later to become the text-book of witch hunters – regarded Dee unfavourably, but allowed him to live out the remainder of his life in relative peace.

John Dee died in 1609 and was laid to rest in Mortlake Church. In the present age some will recall him simply as Queen Elizabeth's astrologer, others may acknowledge his contributions to mathematics and navigation, or even remember him as a pioneer of the public libraries system. Nevertheless, it is in the world of occultism that the spirit of John Dee truly lives on. Certain discoveries made after Dee's death tell of a mysteriously hidden aspect of his life. To these findings we devote the remainder of this volume.

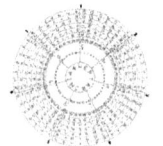

INTRODUCTION

Over four hundred years have elapsed since John Dee transcribed his fair copy of *De Heptarchia Mystica*. Before this, the work existed in embryonic form as a mass of complex and somewhat confusing notes, scattered throughout the early books of his Spiritual Diaries. In the interests of clarity, I have employed Dee's final condensation of the 'Sevenfold Doctrine' as the major text of this volume; to which I have appended an extensive series of notes in an attempt to rectify various shortcomings, and to amplify important points.

The contracted and simplified format of Dee's fair copy seems to have been intended as a basic guide to the system, orientated towards practical experimentation, and possessing striking similarities to many of the grimoires of antiquity. Whether or not Dee actually employed the invocations of the *Heptarchia* in further attempts to communicate with the forty-nine good Angels is uncertain, and certainly not apparent from the scant references to these beings in the later books of *Mysteriorum Libri Quinque* (*Five Books of Mysteries*)[4]. All we can say conclusively is that, apart from minor inconsistencies

---

4. However, two entries in Dee's *Private Diary* imply that the system was used. On 30/31 December 1587, Dee wrote: '*I began to frame myself toward the practice of the Heptagonon of my fourth book*'; and later, on 15 January 1588, he records: '*Heptagoni Mysterium began to be conducted*'.[AT]

THE HEPTARCHIA MYSTICA

and certain obscurities, the Heptarchical text holds together as a unique system of practical occultism, forming the basis of much of Dee's later work.

Fifty-four years after Dee's death, the manuscript of *De Heptarchia Mystica* – together with other items – was discovered by a confectioner named Jones. It had been hidden in a secret drawer concealed within the base of an old cedar wood chest which had been purchased by Jones from a shop in Adle Street, London. Ten years later the manuscript together with a number of additional Dee papers passed into the hands of that champion of the magical arts, Elias Ashmole, who restored them to their place of dignity in the annals of occult history. Ashmole's account regarding the discovery of the manuscripts, and how they subsequently came into his possession, is recorded in his own words on the flyleaf of *Mysteriorum Libri Quinque*. (British Library Sloane MS 3188)

> *Be it remembered, that the 20th of August 1672, I received by the hands of my servant Samuell Story, a part of Dr Dee's Manuscripts all written with his own hand; viz: his conference with Angells, which first began the 22nd of December Ano 1581, and continued to the end of May Ano 1583, where the printed Booke of the remaining conferences (published by Dr Casaubon) begins, and are bound up in this volume.*
>
> *Besides these the Books entitled: The 48 Claves Angelicae, also Liber Scientia Terrestris – Auxilii & Victoria (These two being very individuall Books which the Angels commanded to be burnt and were after restored by them so appears by the printed (Booke) Relations of Dr Dee's Actions with Spirits, pages: 418 & 419.) The Booke entitled De Heptarchia Mystica – Collectanorum Lib: Primus, and a Booke of (Invocations or Calls beginning with*

INTRODUCTION

the Squares, filled with letters about the Black Cross). These four Bookes I have bound up in another volume.[5]

All of which were a few daies before delivered to my said servant for my perusall (I being then at Mr Lillies house, at Hersham in Surry) by my good friend Mr Thomas Wale, one of his Majesties Wardens in the Tower of London. The 5th of Sept. following Mr Wale (having heard of my return to Town) came to my office in the Excise office in Broad Street: and told me he was content to exchange all the afour said Books for one of myne, viz: The Institution of the Garter: to this I agreed and provided one, which I sent him fairly bound, and gilt on the back.

On the 10th of the said Sept: Mr Wale came thither to me again, and brought his wife with him, from her I received the following account of the preservation of these Bookes, until they came to my hands. Viz: that her former husband was one Mr Jones a Confectioner, who formerly dwelt at The Plow in Lumbard street London, and who shortly after they were married, took her with him into Adle street – among the joiners to buy some household stuff when (at the Corner House) they saw a chest of extraordinary neate worke, invited them to buy it. The Master of the shop told them it had been part of the goods of one Mr John Woodall – Chirurgeon (father to Mr Thomas Woodall late Serjant Chirurgeon to his now Majesty King Charles the Second (my intimate friend) and tis very probable he bought it after Dr Dee's death, when his goods were exposed to sale).

Twenty years after this (and about 4 years before the fatall fire of London) her husband and she occasionally removing the chest out of its usuall place, thought they heared some loose things rattle in it toward the right hand end under the box and by some shaking of it were fully satisfied it was so. Hereupon her husband

---

5. British Library Sloane MS 3191.

THE HEPTARCHIA MYSTICA

thrust a piece of Iron into a small crevice at the bottom of the chest and thereupon appeared a private drawer, which being drawn out, therein were found divers Bookes in Manuscript and Papers, together with a little box, and therein a chaplet of olive Beades, and a Cross of the same wood, hanging at the end of them.

They made no great matter of these Books and: because they understood them not; which occasioned their servant maid: to waste about one half of them under pyes, and other like uses, which then discovered they kept the rest more safer.

About two years after the discovery of these Bookes Mr Jones dyed and when the Fire of London hapned though the chest perished in the flames because not easily to be removed, yet the Bookes were taken out and carried with the rest of Mrs Jones her goods into Moore fields, and being brought safely back, she toke care to preserve them: and after marrying the aforesaid Mr Wale, he came to the knowledge of them, and thereupon with her consent, sent to me, as I have before set down.

A strange story indeed; was it a fear of persecution which caused John Dee to hide his most cherished manuscripts during the last years of his life? Or had Dee always concealed his papers and, perhaps, other equipment within the chest out of the sight of prying eyes? Of the content of the spoiled documents we can only speculate and wince with frustration, for although she may have acted as an instrument of fate, the Jones' maid has much to answer for!

During the period in which I was engaged in studying the Dee manuscripts in the British Library, I came across a second copy of *De Heptarchia Mystica* bound up with magical treatises by Caius and Forman (Additional MSS 36,674) entitled *Compendium Heptarchia Mysticae*. The British Library catalogue

INTRODUCTION

note suggests that the manuscript represents a rough draft of Dee's fair copy — Sloane MS 3191, Art. 3 — and is written in the same hand. Apart from minor differences, and the form of the final table, the work appears to be an exact copy of the principal work, even down to the style of writing, which begins chaotically and settles down to a neat precise hand after the first three pages. In addition, the watermark — a hand in the sign of benediction — on each page corresponds exactly to the better known copy of the work. How this version of the *Heptarchia* came to be bound up with the Caius and Forman treatises is somewhat of a mystery, but I feel that here the key may be with Forman.

Simon Forman (1552-1611), an astrologer, magician and practitioner of medicine, probably met with John Dee on July 26, 1604 (from a note in Forman's diary) 'at dinner at Mr Staper's house'[6] . Although their general approach to the magical arts differed — Forman's verging on sorcery and the forbidden —they obviously had much in common and some form of relationship probably developed. It is therefore just possible that Dee introduced Forman to some of his original findings, and even allowed him to take possession of the earlier transcription of *De Heptarchia Mystica*.

According to a note by Montague Summers [7], the 'grimoire' (Ad. MSS 36,674) at one time belonged to Dr John Caius (1510-1573). If this was so, how could *De Heptarchia Mystica*, which was not written until 1582, have formed part of it? At the time of Caius' death Forman was barely twenty-one, so it

---

6. A.L.Rowse. *The Case Books of Simon Forman*, London: Picador Books Ltd, 1976, p. 197. Rowse is mistaken here. There is no evidence that Forman and Dee ever met. It was Forman's friend and pupil, the astrologer and medical practitioner Richard Napier (1559-1634), who Dee saw. They may have met more than once. [AT]

7. Montague Summers. *Witchcraft and black magic*, London: Rider and Co., 1946.

THE HEPTARCHIA MYSTICA

is unlikely that his codex could have been included. Can it be that the Dee manuscript came into the British Museum along with papers belonging to Forman, and was bound up with the Caius treatise at a later date? Whatever the answer, it seems certain that Ashmole possessed one complete version and a partial copy (Ashmole MS 1790, Art 2) of the *Heptarchia*.

It is apparent from the records that have come down to us that John Dee first encountered the enigmatic personality of Edward Kelley on March 10, 1582. It is assumed that Kelley's real name was Talbot, and in the first record of their meeting (*Mysteriorum Liber Primus – The First Book of the Mysteries*) Dee refers to him as such. Nine months later – in November 1582 Dee's references to his scryer change – somewhat abruptly – to 'Edward Kelley'. No convincing explanation for this name change has yet been offered, most authorities considering it to be a convenient let-out for Kelley at a time when his murky past was catching up on him. Whatever the reason for the alias, we do know that the name change took place after certain problems in the Dee-Kelley relationship had been resolved, for the *Quartus Liber Mysteriorum* (*The Fourth Book of the Mysteries*) bears the sub-title P*ost reconciliationem Kellianum* (November 15, 1582), and the name Kelley was employed from this time onward.

Although from time to time Dee had enlisted various other seers, their impact upon Dee's life can be seen as totally insignificant when compared with Kelley. Very little is known regarding Kelley's origin. According to Anthony Wood (*Athena Oxoniensis*, 1813), Edward Kelley appears to have been born at Worcester on August 1, 1555. It is said that his father was an apothecary and of sufficient means to send his son to Oxford

INTRODUCTION

at the age of seventeen. The University records seem to cast some doubt upon this, although several people named Talbot entered during this period. As a profession, Kelley set up as a notary and copyist of wills, and on this ground history accuses him of producing forged title deeds for gain. For this crime he is said to have been pilloried at Lancaster, and afterwards deprived of his ears. Whether or not Kelley in fact suffered this mutilation is uncertain; he is said to have worn a Black skullcap throughout the rest of his life – not unusual in Elizabethan times – but this does nothing to prove the absence of his ears. Arthur Edward Waite, in his preface to *The Alchemical Writings of Edward Kelley*,[8] suggests that the story of Kelley's punishment is likely to be a fabrication perpetuated by Nash, who recorded the events in the *History and Antiquities of Worcester* (London, 1781). In Waite's words:

> *The distinguished position which he held subsequently at the Court of the Emperor Rudolph would scarcely have been possible to a man who had lost his ears. The credulity of royal personages at the end of the seventeenth century may have facilitated many impostures on the part of the alchemists whom they protected, but could scarcely have extended to accepting the philosophical illumination of an adept who had been branded by law.*[9]

According to Waite, Kelley is said to have come into the possession of the fabled *Book of Saint Dunstan* – an alchemical treatise written by the founder of Glastonbury Abbey – together with the White and Red Powders of Projection, while travelling in Wales. [Waite quotes this rather fanciful account from Louis Figuier's *L'Alchemie et les Alchemistes*. The

---

8. A.E. Waite, *The Alchemical Writings of Edward Kelley*. London: Stuart Watkins, 1970. 9. Ibid., p. 20.

THE HEPTARCHIA MYSTICA

story was first related by Daniel Morhof in *Epistola ad Joelum Langelottum de Transmutatione Metallorum*.[10] Morhof claimed to have been told the story by an 'illustrious man' who had heard it from a member of Kelley's family. Morhof identified the 'illustrious man' in his correspondence as the chemist Robert Boyle (1627-1691), whom he had met in 1670. - AT]

The manuscript and two caskets containing the powders were said to have been pillaged from the tomb of a bishop by a fanatical Protestant mob, and subsequently exchanged with an innkeeper for a quantity of wine. The innkeeper – not understanding the significance of these items – is alleged to have sold the curios to Kelley for one guinea. Extant versions of this tale cast little light on the truth of the matter; it is however quite likely that Kelley possessed something of this nature, as Dee makes mention of certain powders and a scroll in various diary sections.[11] Unlike Dee, Kelley was not a literary man, his two short treatises entitled *The Philosopher's Stone* and *The Theatre of Terrestrial Astronomy* (published Hamburg, 1676) being his only contributions to posterity.

[These two alchemical tracts were written during his second term of imprisonment under Emperor Rudolph II in Castle Hněvín, located on a precipitous hill overlooking the town of Most (German: Brüx) in Northern Bohemia. It seems that Kelley was held prisoner in the castle for failing to produce the transmutation of metals which he had promised the Emperor. It was there in his forty-second year that Kelley met his death on 1st November 1597. The date is derived from the prison records, which show the daily payment made

---

10. Published in *Bibliotheca Chemica Curiosa*, ed. by Jean-Jacques Manget, Geneva: Chouet, 1702. [AT] 11. See Appendix D for more information from Dee's diaries about finding these items. [REC]

INTRODUCTION

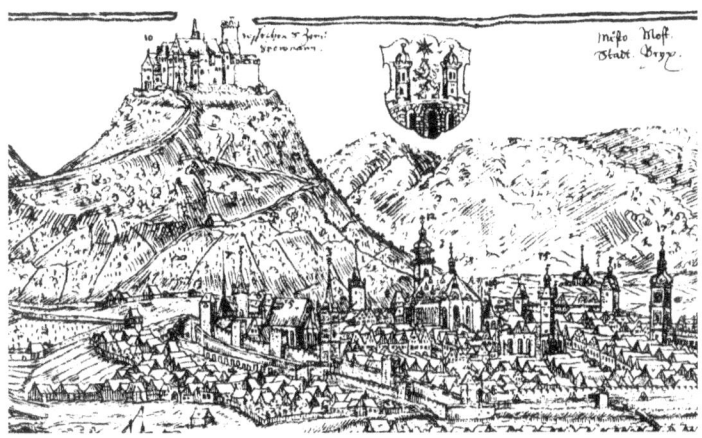

Most and Castle Hněvín. Contemporary woodcut by Jan Willenberg, c.1602

by his wife Joanna Kelley for his upkeep, including meals, a personal servant and four guards. The payments ceased after 1st November 1597 and nothing more verifiable is heard of him. [12] In an attempt to escape from his captors, it appears he had fallen from the castle ramparts and shortly after died from his injuries. Another account relates his injuries were so severe that he took his own life with poison. - REC]

Kelley's dark reputation as a necromancer stems largely from an account in John Weaver's *Discourse of Ancient Funeral Monuments* (London, 1631). Weaver relates how Edward Kelley and one Paul Waring by way of incantations caused the spirit of a deceased person to return from the grave. The operation is held to have taken place in the yard of Lawe (or Lowe) Chapel[13] near Walton-le-Dale in the county of Lancaster. A well-known engraving of the scene was produced in the second edition of Ebenezer Sibly's *Illustration of the Occult Sciences*.

---

12. Sviták, Ivan. *Malostranská Sapfo*, Prague: Isis, 1994. pp. 28-31. [REC] 13. Today St Leonard's Church, Walton-le-Dale, near Preston, Lancashire. [REC]

THE HEPTARCHIA MYSTICA

Postcard of Most/Brüx, c. 1939 (Collection: R. Cousins). The historic old town of Most was demolished in the 1960s to make way for the surface mining of lignite. A decision now regretted. [REC]

Kelley and Paul Waring at Walton-Le-Dale, from Ebenezer Sibly's *A New and Complete Illustration of the Occult Sciences*, 1806.

INTRODUCTION

The Sibly engraving depicts two men standing within a magic circle; one holds aloft a torch, the other reads from a book while pointing to various mystical characters with a wand. Before the two stands the spirit of the deceased dressed in its grave-clothes and seeming to speak. This engraving over the years has caused much confusion, ignorant commentators mistaking Kelley's companion to be John Dee.[14] Although

Statue of Kelley by Daniel Vlasák (2003) at Castle Hněvín, Most.[15]

John Dee was probably aware of Edward Kelley's somewhat nefarious background, it seems to have had little influence upon his assessment of the seer's clairvoyant abilities. From the outset, the visions reported by Kelley far outstripped anything

14. Kelley's companion was local man Paul Waring from nearby Dove Cotes, Clayton Brook. [REC] 15. Detail from the original colour photograph *'Socha Kellyho na Hněvíně (Most)' (Statue of Edward Kelley in Castle Hněvín)* created 31 May 2013 by Gortyna, CC-BY-SA-3.0 via Wikimedia Commons . Link to file: https://commons.wikimedia.org/wiki/File:Kelley_Hn%C4%9Bv%C3%ADn.jpg [REC]

THE HEPTARCHIA MYSTICA

which had been revealed by his previous scryer (Barnabas Saul), and a definite system of working soon emerged.

Without doubt Kelley was a man of remarkable talents, often possessed with the 'gift of tongues' and – if we are to believe Dee's accounts – capable of producing physical manifestations. History has not always given Kelley an easy passage, branding him always as the rogue, the charlatan, and the wife-swapper who lost his ears.[16] Yet those of us who have examined the wealth of the Dee manuscripts in detail can only wonder if there is not much more to this strangely powerful personality who shaped a whole epoch of magical history.

When we consider that *De Heptarchia Mystica* represents possibly the only true example of a complete magical system to be found in the Dee papers, it is difficult to see why it has been almost totally neglected by generations of occultists.

Highly synthetic and fanciful adaptations of Dee's later 'Enochian' material were incorporated into the *Knowledge Papers* of the Hermetic Order of the Golden Dawn, with little justification. But apart from a garbled extract in a notebook belonging to F. L. Gardner, I can find no evidence to suggest that the Heptarchical system was ever investigated. In recent years, a well-known Dallas-based American foundation produced a beautifully executed series of printed diagrams of Dee's Sigillum Æmeth, Holy Table, Enochian Alphabet and seven seals. Unfortunately, all of these offerings must be considered to be practically useless owing to serious design errors. The American version of Sigillum Æmeth follows that published by Crowley (*The Equinox*, Volume 1, No. 7) and incorporates a host of rather obvious mistakes; while their 'Holy Table' repeats

---

16. For details of this exchange of wives, see *A True and Faithful Relation*, pp. 468-9. [RT]

INTRODUCTION

Casaubon's oddly transposed rendering (see Appendix A, note 6 of the present volume). In addition to this we find an Enochian Alphabet marred by nonsensical Golden Dawn grammatical rules, and above all a totally impossible series of seals which suffer from the artist's inability to distinguish between Dee's lower-case b and the number 6! Thus we have a prime example of the 'blind leading the blind', and the need for properly qualified research into the complex and confusing area of Elizabethan magic.

The illustrations and text of the present work do not suffer from the above defects, the artist and author working in close collaboration and drawing entirely from original sources. A few obscure areas still remain, but in every case these have been strongly indicated in the text. Where alternatives are possible, both versions have been carefully represented in order that the reader has the opportunity to judge for himself.

The main text of this edition of *De Heptarchia Mystica* has been compiled from a painstaking collation of the two extant Dee texts (BL Sloane MS 3191, Additional MS 36,674), with peripheral notes and explanations taken from *Mysteriorum Libri Quinque*. (BL Sloane MS 3188 and BL Sloane MS 3677 – Ashmole's copy). Diagrams have in all cases been taken from the original texts, Casaubon's printed versions only being referred to by way of comparison.

At this point I feel that it would be of value to mention the well-known Rudd treatise contained in Harley Manuscript 6482. Entitled *Tabula Sancta cum Tablis Enochi*, article two of the manuscript purports to explain the structure and application the seven tablets used in conjunction with Dee's Holy Table (see Appendix A, note 9). According to Dr Rudd, each tablet represents elaborate conclaves of spirits – some good, others evil

THE HEPTARCHIA MYSTICA

– together with details regarding the number of times certain of these spirits are to be invocated. Rudd's line of reasoning is, to say the least, hard to follow. The method employed by Dee and Kelley to obtain these tablets or tables forbids the validity of Rudd's explanation. In addition, as Dee states that each table is 'proper to every King and Prince in their order', we must conclude even the sequence in which Rudd evaluates each square to be incorrect. The first tablet Rudd names '*Tabula Lunae*' (Table of the Moon), yet Dee places its King (Baligon) under the rule of Venus.

Rudd's second tablet – which is Dee's seventh – is ascribed to Mercury instead of the Luna influence of Blvmaza, and so on. The first table of the Rudd codex is, in his opinion, composed mainly of the names and sigils of Goetic demons – taken from *The Lemegeton* – a concept which John Dee would find impossible to countenance. In conclusion I feel that we can safely disregard Dr Rudd's hypotheses with regard to these matters and leave the secret of these mysterious tablets with John Dee and the Angels.[17] A final note might be added to the effect that A. E. Waite seemed to consider Dr Thomas Rudd a fictitious character, the alter ego of one Peter Smart, who assembled the Rudd collection in the years 1712-14. The last word on Rudd I leave therefore to Waite who writes on page 101 of his *Brotherhood of the Rosy Cross*:

> *I conclude that the Rudd MSS might be commended to the notice of the American Rosy Cross in some of its developments as an*

---

17. It's clear that Rudd's sole source of information was the diagram of the Holy Table in *A True and Faithful Relation*. He took the ensigns from that and invented meanings, just as he attributed the geomantic symbols to some of the angelic letters taken from the periphery of the table. Nothing suggests he understood what he was dealing with. [AT]

INTRODUCTION

early example of its own dispositions in the art of occult fraud.[18]

Throughout the present text I have, for the most part, adhered to the original phrasing and punctuation of Dee's fair copy in an effort to convey to the reader its atmosphere of unique antiquity. The expansions and elaborations of textual points given in Appendix A have been submitted in order to surmount, to the best of my ability, various difficulties arising from the archaic and contracted form of Dee's original manuscript. In addition, Appendix B has been included to deal with other matters of importance not specifically indicated in the main text. It is hoped that the inclusion of these items will enhance the value of the work and perhaps provide useful leads to serious researchers.

In offering this edition of John Dee's *De Heptarchia Mystica* to the world, a preliminary goal has been achieved which, it is hoped, may pave the way for further advancements in this intriguing area of study. I am sure that others will pursue these studies to a greater depth than has been immediately possible, and in time the many paradoxical elements in Dee's text will finally offer up their secrets. On a practical level, a certain revival of interest in Dee's Heptarchical magic has been noted. Whether or not the spirits will welcome this invasion of their four hundred year repose remains to be seen.

Robert Turner
August 1983

---

18. A.E. Waite. *Brotherhood of the Rosy Cross* , New York: University Books, 1961.

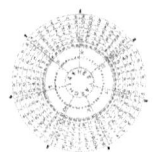

DE HEPTARCHIA MYSTICA A° 1582

The whole world is arranged in sevens, of all that is brought to life and is born. Indeed there are seven first born princes of the angels whose power is greatest. [19]
Clemens Alex: stromi (Lib: 6) [1] [20]
D.

---

19. *In septenariis totus Mundus circumagitur omnium quae et viva gignutur, et quae nascuntur. Septem quidem sunt (quorum est maxima potentia) Primogeniti Angelorum principes – etc.* 20. Annexed numbers in square brackets refer to notes and diagrams contained in Appendix A. Translations from Latin in the text are given in italics.

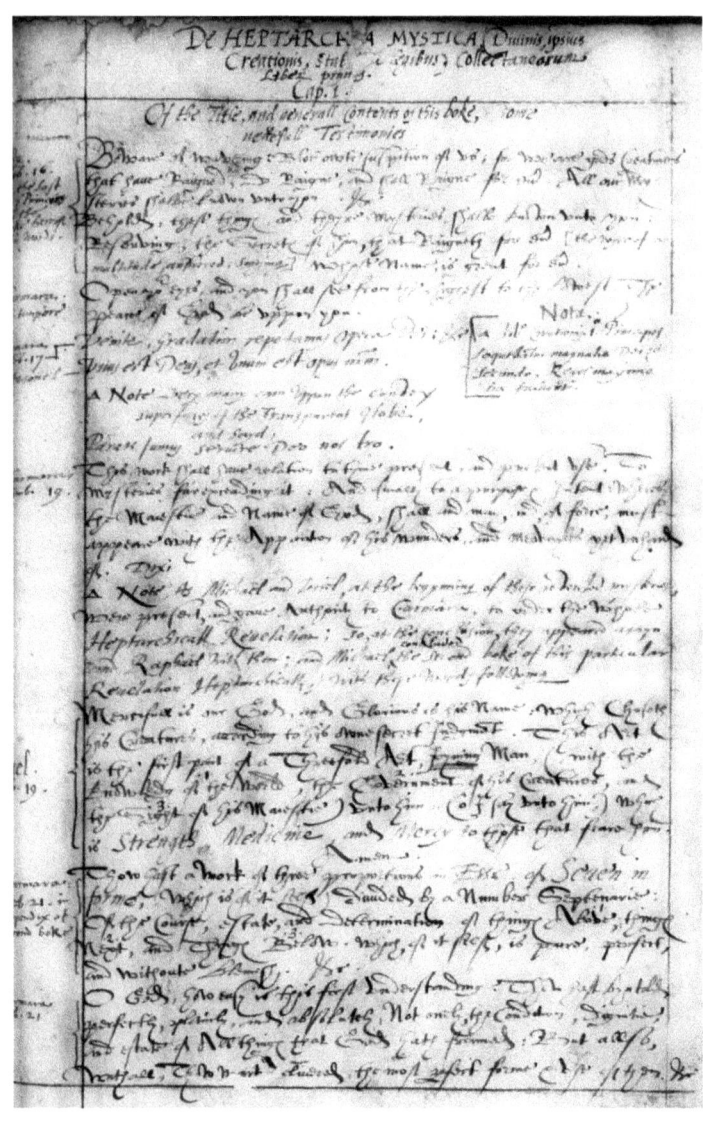

De Heptarchia Mystica in Dee's hand.
© British Library Board (BL Sloane MS 3191, Folio 33r.)

DE HEPTARCHIA MYSTICA
Divinis ipsius Creationis, Stab... Legibus
(The divine laws of creation itself)

COLLECTANEORUM LIBER PRIMUS
(Book 1 of the Collectanea)

CAP.1
OF THE TITLE AND GENERAL CONTENTS OF THIS BOOK, SOME NEEDFUL TESTIMONIES

A° 1582. November 16,
Bralges: the last of
the 7 Princes, concluding
the First Book hereof with these words:

D.

Beware of wavering: blot out suspicion of us, for we are God's creatures that have reigned, do reign and shall reign forever. All our mysteries shall be known unto you, etc.

Behold, these things and their mysteries shall be known unto you: reserving the secrets of him that reigneth for ever, (the voice of a multitude answered saying) 'Whose name is great for ever'.

KING CARMARA: eodem tempore (*at the same time*):
Open your eyes and you shall see from the highest to the lowest. The peace of God be upon you.

THE HEPTARCHIA MYSTICA

NOVEMBER 17:
Venite, gradatim repetamus Opera Dei, etc. (*Come, let us gradually seek the works of God.*)

PRINCE HAGONEL:
Unus est Deus, et unum est opum nostrum. (*There is one God, and there is one work of ours.*)

D. *Note:* Libro Creationis 1° principes loquebantur magnalia Dei et secundo reges maxime hoc faciunt. (*In the first book of creation, the Princes spoke of God's mighty works and in the second, the Kings mostly do this.*)

D. *Note:* Very many came upon the convex superfices of the transparent globe and said: Parati sumus servire Deo nostro. (*We are ready to serve our God.*)

KING CARMARA:
NOVEMBER 19:
This work shall have relation to present time and present use, to mysteries far exceeding it: and finally to a purpose and intent whereby the majesty and name of God shall and may, and, of force, must appear, with the apparition of his wonders and marvels yet unheard of. Dixi. (*I have spoken.*)

D. *Note*: As Michael and Uriel at the beginning of these revealed mysteries were present and gave authority to Carmara to order the whole Heptarchical revelation, so, at the conclusion, they appeared again and Raphael with them: and Michael concluded the second book (of this particular revelation Heptarchical) with these words following:

CAP. 1

MICHAEL:
NOVEMBER 19:
Merciful is our God and glorious is his name which chooseth his creatures according to his own secret judgement. This art is the 1st part of a threefold art, joining man (with the knowledge of this world, the government of his creatures, and the sight of his majesty) unto him (O I say unto him) which is strength, medicine and mercy to those that fear him.

KING CARMARA:
NOVEMBER 21, in the appendix of ye second book:
Thou hast a work of three proportions in essence — of seven in form. Which is (of itself) divided by a number septenary. Of the course, estate, and determination of things above, things next, and things below: which of itself is pure, perfect, and without blemish, etc.

KING CARMARA:
NOVEMBER 21:
O God, how easy is this first understanding. Thou hast been told perfectly, plainly and absolutely, not only the condition, dignity and estate of all things that God hath formed; but also, withall, thou wert delivered the most perfect form and use of them, etc.

KING CARMARA:
NOVEMBER 17:
Even as God is just, his judgements true, his mercies unspeakable, so are we the true messengers of God, and our words are true in his mercies forever. Glory, O glory, be to thee, most high God.

THE HEPTARCHIA MYSTICA

MICHAEL:
April 29, A° 1582:
Now you touch on the world and the doings on earth. Now we show to you the lower world. The governors that work and rule under God. By whom you may have power to work such things as shall be to God's glory, profit of your country, and the knowledge of his creatures. So we proceed to one God, one knowledge, one operation. Venite filiae (*Come daughters*), behold these tables: herein lie their names that work under God on earth. Not of the wicked but of the ANGELS OF LIGHT. The whole government doth consist in the hands of 49 (in God his power, strength, mercy and justice), whose names are here evident, excellent and glorious. Mark these tables, mark them, record them to your comfort. This is the first knowledge. Here shall you have wisdom. Halleluyah.

Mighty and omnipotent art thou, O God, God, God, amongst thy creatures, thou fillest all things with thy excellent foresight. Thy glory be amongst us forever. (**D.** *Amen*)

URIEL:
April 29, A° 1582:
The fountain of wisdom is opened. Nature shall be known. Earth with her secrets disclosed. The elements with their powers judged. Behold I teach: there are 49 Angels, glorious and excellent, appointed for the government of all earthly actions: which 49 do work and dispose the will of the Creator: limited from the beginning in strength, power and glory. THESE SHALL BE SUBJECT UNTO YOU, in the name and by invocating the name of God, who doth lighten, dispose and comfort you.

CAP. 1

KING CARMARA:

NOVEMBER 19, of King Bobogel, his princely ministers:
What doth the Heaven behold; or the earth contain, that is not or may be subdued, formed and made by these? What learning grounded upon wisdom with the excellencies in nature cannot they manifest.

One in Heaven they know:
One and all in man they know:
One and all in Earth they know.

Measure heaven by a part (my meaning is by these few) let God be glorified, his name be praised, his creation well taken, and his creatures well used.

URIEL:

MAY 5, A° 1583:
He that standeth in the midst of the globe signifieth nature: whereupon in the first point is the use and practice of this work. That is to say, as concerning the first part, for it is said:

The book containeth three kinds of knowledge:
The knowledge of God truly.
The number and doings of his Angels perfectly.
The beginning and ending of Nature substantially.

CAP. 2
OF JOHN DEE, HIS PRINCIPAL, AND IN MANNER PECULIAR INTEREST TO EXORCISE THE DOCTRINE HEPTARCHICAL

URIEL:
A° 1582, NOVEMBER 11:
Ultima est haec aetas nostra, quae tibi revelata erit. (This is our last age, which shall be revealed to you.)

MICHAEL:
The mysteries of God hath a time; and behold thou art provided for that time.

HAGONEL:
NOVEMBER 16:
The Sons of Light (**D.** *Amen*), and their Sons are subject unto my commandment. This is a mystery; I have spoken of it. Note it thoroughly. By them thou shalt work marvels. There are kings false and unjust, whose power as I have subverted (*or augmented*) and destroyed, so shalt thou. The second assembly were the governors of the earth. Whose glory (if they be good) the weapons we have taught thee will augment, and consequently (if they be evil) pervert.

CAP. 2

BORNOGO:
November 16:
I am Bornogo: this is my seal: this is my true character. What thou desirest me, shall be fulfilled. Glory to God.

BEFAFES:
Behold, behold, lo behold. My mighty power consisteth in this. Learn wisdom by my words. This is wrought for thy erudition, what I instruct thee from God. Look unto thy charge truly: thou art yet dead. Thou shalt be revived. But oh, bless God truly. The blessing that God giveth me, I will bestow upon thee by permission. O, how mighty is our God which walked on the waters, which sealed me with his name, whose glory is without end. Thou hast written me but yet dost thou not know me. Use me, in the name of God: I shall at the time appointed be ready. I will manifest the works of the seas and the miracles of the deep shall be known.

KING CARMARA:
November 17:
Behold thou desirest, and art sick with desire: I am the disposer, though not the composer of God's medicines: thou desirest to be comforted and strengthened in thy labours, I minister unto thee the strength of God. What I say is not of myself; neither that which is said to me, is of themselves but is said of him which liveth for ever. These mysteries hath God lastly, and His great mercies granted unto thee. I have answered thy doubting minds. Thou shalt be glutted, yea, thou shalt be filled, yea thou shalt swell and be puffed up with the perfect knowledge of God's mysteries in His mercies. Abuse them not. Be faithful. Use mercy. God shall enrich thee. Banish wrath. It was the first

THE HEPTARCHIA MYSTICA

and the greatest commandment. I reign by him, and live by him, which reigneth and liveth for ever.

Marginal Note: Annael gave me that commandment A° 1581, in the preface as it were of all these actions. (**D**.)

KING CARMARA:
NOVEMBER 17:
I have showed thee perfectly. Behold I teach thee again. O how merciful is God that revealeth so great secrets to flesh and blood. Thou hast 42 letters. Thy tables last contain so many, etc.

KING CARMARA: eodem tempore (*at the same time*):
When thou wilt work for anything appertaining to the estate of a good king, thou must call upon him, which is their Prince. Secondly the ministers of his power, are six etc.

KING CARMARA: eodem tempore (*at the same time*):
In outward sense my words are true. I speak now of the use of one of the first, that I spake of, or manifested yesterday. Said I not and showed I not, which had the government of Princes, for as it is a mystery to a further matter, so it is a purpose to a present use. If it rule worldly Princes, how much more shall it work with the Princes of Creation. Thou desirest use. I teach use. And yet the Art is to the further understanding of all sciences, that are past, present, or yet to come. Fruit hath further virtue, than only in the eating. Gold his further condition, property and quality, than in melting or common use. Kings there are in Nature. Thou art dignified, etc. . . .

CAP. 2

THE RING

KING CARMARA: eodem tempore *(at the same time)*:
Last of all, thy Ring, which was appointed thee; with the Lamyne comprehending the form of thy own name, which is to be made in perfect gold as is aforesaid. [2]

KING CARMARA:
Thou shalt be comforted, but respect the world to come. Whereunto thou art provided and for what end: and in what time. Serve God truly, serve him justly. Great care is to be had with those that meddle with Princes' affairs. Much more consideration with whom thou shalt meddle or use any practice. But God hath shadowed thee from destruction. He preserveth his faithful, and shadoweth the just, with a shield of honour. None shall enter into the knowledge of these mysteries with thee, but this worker (i.e. Edward Kelley). Thy estate with the Prince now reigning shall shortly be amended. Her favour increased with the good wills of divers that are now deceased. Thy hand shall shortly be their help; and thou shalt do wonderful and many benefits (to the augmenting of God's glory) for thy country. Finally, God doth enrich thee with knowledge, and of thyself hath given thee understanding of these worldly vanities. He is merciful, and we his good creatures, neither have, do, nor will forget thee. God doth bless you both; whose mercy, goodness, and grace, I pronounce and utter upon you.

KING BOBOGEL:
NOVEMBER 19:
I have said Dee, Dee, Dee, at length, but not too late.

THE HEPTARCHIA MYSTICA

D. *Note*: King Bobogel said this of my attaining to such mysteries as the Ministers under him made show of.

KING CARMARA:
NOVEMBER 20:
Lo! thus thou seest the glory of God's creatures. Whom thou mayst use with consideration of the day, their King, their Prince and his character. The King and Prince govern for the whole day. The rest according to the six parts of the day. Use them to the glory, praise, and honour of Him which created them, to the laud and praise of His Majesty.

KING BYNEPOR:
NOVEMBER 20:
Write this reverently, note it with submission. What I speak hath not been revealed: not in these last times of the second last world, etc. Thou shalt work marvellous marvellously by my workmanship in the highest.

KING BNASPOL:
NOVEMBER 20:
Unto my Prince, my subject, are delivered the keys of the mysteries of earth. All these are Angels that govern under him, etc: so use them, they are and shall be at thy commandment.

KING BNAPSEN: [21]
NOVEMBER 20:
By me thou shalt cast out the power of wicked spirits. By me, thou shalt know the doings and practices of evil men. And more than may be spoken or uttered to man.

21. In the manuscript, Dee incorrectly spells 'Bnapsen' here as 'Bnaspen'. [REC]

CAP. 2

KING CARMARA:
NOVEMBER 21:

O quanta est hominis infirmitas et corruptio, qui Angelis, idque suis bonis, fidem autem Deo vix habet? Omnia Mundana faecas Mundi corruptiones in se habent. Deus noster, Deus noster, Deus (inquam) ille noster, verus cum veris suis Angelis eique servientibus, semper verus est: Pete quae vis. Dixi: et quod dixi, Obumbratum est veritate, justitia et perfectione.

Ecce . . . holding up the meet rod.

Hic . . . Pointing to the end of the rod.

per hoc . . . Pointing to the middle of it.

Eta mensurae fine nos, nostramque mensurabis potestatem. Age (inquam) Quid vis, obscurumenim nihil est, quod per ilium [E.K.] recepisti.

(O how great is the infirmity and corruption of man that has faith in angels and their good works but scarcely at all in God. All worldly things contain the corruption of the world within them. Our God, our God, that true God of ours (I say) with his true angels and those that serve him is always true. Seek what you wish. I have spoken and what I have said is cloaked in truth, justice and perfection.

And from the end of the measure you will measure us and our power. And we will do what you wish, for nothing is obscure that you have received through him [E.K.].)

THE RECEPTACLE

KING CARMARA:
NOVEMBER 21:

One thing is yet wanting, a meet receptacle. There is yet wanting a stone. One there is most excellent, hid in the secret of the

THE HEPTARCHIA MYSTICA

depth, etc. in the uttermost part of the Roman possession, etc. Lo, the mighty hand of God is upon thee, etc. Thou shalt prevail with it, with Kings and with all the Creatures of the world; whose beauty (in virtue) shall be more worth than the kingdoms of the earth. Go towards it and take it up. Keep it secret. Let no mortal hand touch it but thy own.

Thy character must have the names of the five Angels (written in the midst of Sigillum Æmeth) graven upon the other side in a circle, in the midst whereof must the stone be (which was also brought). Wherein thou shalt at all times behold privately to thyself, the state of God's people throughout the whole earth. [3]

Marginal Note: A° 1583, May 5.
IL: cuius nomen est primu Filiorum Lucis: IL ponitur in character ipsii Baligon sive Carmara Regis. (*whose name is the first of [the Sons of] the Sons of Light: IL is placed in the character [Seal] of Baligon or King Carmara himself*) [22]

RAPHAEL:
March 26, A° 1583:
Go and thou shalt receive, tarry and you shall receive. Sleep and you shall see. But watch and your eyes shall be fully opened. One thing which is the ground and element of thy desire, is already perfected, etc. Out of seven (or heaven) thou hast been instructed of the lesser part most perfectly.

All those before spoken of are subject to thy call of friendship at any time, thou mayst see them and know what thou wilt.

---

22. IL is a really conjoined E and L and is sometimes written as EL, as it is in the seal of Baligon (see Cap. 4 and the entry for 21 March 1582). [REC]

CAP. 2

Everyone (to be short) shall at all times and seasons show thee direction in anything.

One thing I answer thee for all offices. Thou hast in subjection all offices. Use them when it pleaseth thee and as thy instruction hath been.

URIEL:
APRIL 23, A° 1583:
The Lord saith, I have hardened the heart of one of you: yea, I have hardened him, as the flint, and burnt him together with the ashes of a cedar. To the intent he may be proved just in my work and great in the strength of my glory. Neither shall his mind consent to the wickedness of iniquity: for from iniquity I have chosen him, to be a first Earthly Witness of my Dignity.

MICHAEL:
his manner of apparition:
D. *Note*: Uriel came in again and another with him, and jointly they two said together:

Praise God for ever. Glorify God for ever. And now Uriel stood behind and the other sat down in the chair, with the sword in his right hand. All his head glistened like the sun; the hair of his head was long, he had wings and all his lower parts seemed to be with feathers. He had a robe over his body, and a great light in his left hand.

MICHAEL:
MARCH 11, A° 1582, he said:
"*We are blessed from the beginning, and blessed be the name of God for ever.*"

THE HEPTARCHIA MYSTICA

D. *Note*: An innumerable company of Angels were about him, and Uriel did lean on the Square Table by. He that sat in the chair said then:

"*Go forward, God hath blessed thee.*
I will be thy guide.
Thou shalt attain unto thy searching.
The world BEGINS WITH THY DOINGS.
Praise God.
The Angels under my power shall be at thy commandment.
Thou shalt see me.
I will be seen of thee,
And I will direct thy living and conversation.
Put up thy pen."

MICHAEL:
March 14, the Ring:

(**Dee:** Now Michael thrust out his right arm with the sword, and bade the scryer to look. Then the sword did seem to cleave in two and a great fire flamed out of it vehemently. Then he took a Ring out of the flame of his sword and gave it to Uriel, and said: "*The strength of God is unspeakable, praised be God for ever and ever.*")

Dee:
Then Uriel did make curtsy to him.

MICHAEL:
After this sort must the Ring be. Note it. I will reveal thee this Ring which was never revealed since the death of Salomon, with whom I was present. I was present with him IN STRENGTH AND MERCY. Lo, this it is. This it is wherewith all miracles and divine works and wonders were wrought by

CAP. 2

SALOMON. This it is which I have revealed unto thee. This it is which philosophy dreameth of. This it is which the Angels scarce know. This it is, and blessed be his name for ever, etc. Yea, his name shall be blessed for ever.

Dee:
Then he laid the Ring down upon the Table, and said:
(**D.** *Note*: I noted the manner of the Ring in all points.)

Dee:
After that he threw the Ring down upon the Table, and it seemed to fall through the Table.

MICHAEL:
So shall it do at thy commandment: WITHOUT THIS THOU SHALT DO NOTHING.

Blessed be his name that encompasseth all things: wonders are in him, and his name is wonderful, his name worketh wonders from generation to generation.

D. *Note*: Then he brought in the seal which he showed the other day; and he opened his sword, and bade the scryer read: and he read: EMETH — then the sword closed up again: and Michael said: "*This I do open unto thee; because thou marvelled at SIGILLUM DEI: this is the name of the Seal which is blessed for ever. This is the Seal itself: this is Holy: this is pure: this is for ever. Amen*".

MICHAEL:
MARCH 15, A° 1582:
As truly as I was with Salomon, so truly will I be with thee: etc. I was with Salomon, in all his works and wonders. Use me, in the name of God FOR ALL OCCASIONS.

CAP. 3

SOME REMEMBRANCES OF THE FURNITURE AND CIRCUMSTANCES NECESSARY IN THE EXERCISE HEPTARCHICAL

KING CARMARA:
IN THE PRESENCE OF **MICHAEL**, A° 1582,
NOVEMBER 17TH:

First cast thine eye unto the general Prince, Governor, or Angel that is principal in this world, then place my name whom thou hast already: then the name of him that was showed thee yesterday (with the short coat). Then his power with the rest of his six perfect ministers. With these thou shalt work to a good end. All the rest thou mayst use to God's glory, for every one of them shall minister to thy necessities.

Moreover – when thou workest thy feet must be placed upon these tables which thou seest written last, comprehending 42 letters and names. [4] But with this consideration: that the first character (which is the first of the 7 in thy former book) be placed upon the top of the Table, which thou wast and art and shall be commanded to have and use. Last of all, the Ring which was appointed thee with the Lamyne comprehending the form of thy own name which is to be made in perfect gold as aforesaid. Even as God is just, his judgements true, his mercies unspeakable, so are we the true messengers of God and our words are true in his mercy forever. Glory, O glory be to thee O most high God.

KING CARMARA:
NOVEMBER 20:
Lo, thus thou seest the glory of God's creatures whom thou mayst use with the consideration of the day, their King, their Prince and his character: the King and the Prince govern for the whole day. The rest according to the six parts of the day. Use them to the praise, glory and honour of him which created them, to the laud and praise of his majesty.

KING CARMARA:
NOVEMBER 21:
The characters of the Kings are in the globe and of the Princes in the heptagonon.

PRINCE HAGONEL:
NOVEMBER 16:
The Sons of Light and their Sons are subject unto my commandment. This is a mystery. I have spoken it. Note it thoroughly. They are my servants. By them thou shalt work marvels. MY TIME IS YET TO COME. The Operation of the Earth is subject to my power and I am the first of the twelve: my seal is called Barees: and here it is. [5]

HAGONEL: eodem tempore (*at the same time*):
In his name with my name, by my character, and the rest of my ministers, are these things brought to pass.

THE HEPTARCHIA MYSTICA

1. These that lie here, those are witches, enchanters, deceivers and blasphemers. And finally all they that use nature with abuse: and dishonour him which reigneth for ever.

2. The second assembly were the Governors of the Earth whose glory if they be good, the weapons which we have taught thee will augment: and consequently (if they be evil) will pervert.

3. The third assembly are those which taste of God's mysteries and drink of the juice of nature: whose minds are divided. Some with eyes looking towards heaven, the rest to the centre of the earth: Ubi non gloria, nec Bonitas, nec Bonum est. (*Where there is neither glory, nor goodness, nor good.*) It is wrought (I say) it is wrought for thy understanding by the Seven of the Seven which were the Sons of Sempiternity whose names thou hast written and recorded to God's glory.

Dee. *Note*: Prince Bvtmono said this but the office is under King Bnaspol whose Prince is Blisdon. The mystery of this I know not yet: for Blisdon will be found to be the proper minister of King Bnaspol, vide A° 1583 May 5th of the making of Mensa foederis (*the table of the contract*), and of my golden Lamyne. [6]

HAGONEL:

Mark this: all spirits inhabiting within the earth where their habitation is of force or not of will (except the middest of myself which I know not), are subject to the power hereof (pointing to his seal), with this you shall govern, with this you shall unlock: with this (in the name of him who reigneth) you shall discover her entrails.

CAP. 3

KING CARMARA:
NOVEMBER 17:
When thou wilt work anything appertaining to the state of a good King, thou must call upon him which is their Prince.

    Secondly, the Ministers of his power are six whose names contain 7 letters apiece and thy tables do manifest by whom in general, or by any one of them in particular, thou shalt work for any intent or purpose. As concerning the letters, particularly, they do concern the names of 42, which 42 in general, or one of them, do and can work the destruction, hindrance or annoyance of the estate, condition, or degree (as well for body as Government) of any wicked or ill living Prince, etc.

    Venito Bobogel Rex et Princeps Nobilitatis. Venito cum Ministris: Venito (inquam) venito cum satellitibus tuis, munitus. *(Let Bobogel come, King and Prince of nobility. Let him come with his Ministers. Come (I say) come defended by your attendants.)*

(**Dee:** This I note for the form of calling.)

KING BOBOGEL, TO HIS PRINCE:
Veni Princeps 7 Principum, qui sunt Aquarum Principes: ego sum Rex potens et mirabilis in aquis, cuius potestas, est aquarum visceribus. (*Come, Prince of the 7 Princes who are Princes of the Waters. I am the King, mighty and marvellous in waters, whose power is in the depths of the waters.*)

KING CARMARA:
Venito veni (inquam) adesto. Veni Rex. O Rex, Rex, Rex Aquarum. Venito (inquam) magna est tua, major autem mea potestas. Vitam dedit Deus omnibus creaturis, venite. Veni ignis: veni vita mortalium (inquam) venito adesdum. Regnat Deus,

THE HEPTARCHIA MYSTICA

O venite. Nam unus ille regnat, et est vita viventium. (*Come, come (I say) be present. Come, King. O King, King, King of the Waters. Come (I say). Great is your power, but mine is greater. God gave life to all creatures, come. Come, fire: come life of mortals (I say) come hither. God reigns, O come. For he alone rules and is life to the living.*)

KING CARMARA, also **BALIGON:** eodem temporare (*at the same time*):
Venite, ubi, nulla quies sed stridor dentium. Venite vos, qui sub mea estis potestate. (*Come where there is no peace but the gnashing of teeth. Come you who are under my power.*)

KING CARMARA:
NOVEMBER 21:
Behold every one of these Princes must have his peculiar Table.

URIEL:
MAY 5, A° 1583:
Thy character must have the names of the five Angels (written in the midst of Sigillum Æmeth) graven upon the other side in a circle. In the midst whereof must the stone be which was also brought, whereon thou shalt at all time behold (privately to thyself) the state of God's people, through the whole Earth.

The 4 feet of the table must have 4 hollow things of sweet wood whereupon they must stand. Within the hollowness whereof their seals may be kept – unperished. ONE MONTH IS ALL FOR THE USE THEREOF. [7]

The silk must be of divers colours: the most changeable that can be gotten. For who is able to behold the Glory of the Seat of God?

CAP. 3

Dee. *Note*: The Character or Lamyne for me was noted (A° 1582 November 17) that it should contain some token of my name: and now in this accounted the true character of dignification, I perceived no peculiar mark of letters of my name. [8]

URIEL:
The form in every corner considereth thy name.

Dee:
You mean there to be a certain shadow of Delta?

URIEL:
Well.

Dee:
What is the use of the 7 Tables (like arms) and from what ground are they framed or derived?

URIEL:
They are the Ensigns of the Creation wherewith all they were created by God: known only by their acquaintance and the manner of their doings. [9]

Dee:
Have I rightly applied the days to the Kings?

URIEL:
The days are rightly applied to the Kings.

Dee:
The characters and words annexed to the Kings' names in the outer circumference of the great circle or globe, how are they to be used?

THE HEPTARCHIA MYSTICA

URIEL:
They are to be painted on sweet wood: and so to be held in thy hand, as thou shalt have cause to use them.[23] [10]

IL (**Dee.** *Note*: the first of the 7 Sons of Sons of Light):
APRIL 28, A° 1583:
Sigillum Æmeth is to be set in the middle of the Table. Grace, mercy and peace be unto the lively branches of his flourishing Kingdoms. And strong thou art in thy glory which dost unite the secret parts of thy lively workmanship and that therefore the weak understanding of man. Herein is thy power and magnificence opened unto man. And why? Because thy divinity and secret power is here shut up in Numero tenario, and quaternario. A quo principium, et fundamentum omne hujus est tui sanctissimi Operis. (*...the number three and four, from which is the beginning and all the foundation of this, your most holy work.*)

IL:
Dee. *Note*: the living and semper
adherent to King Baligon,
and his name is expressed
in his character [or Seal]:
VIDE NOVEMBER 21 A° 1582:
For if thou (O God) be wonderful and incomprehensible in thine own substance, it must needs follow that thy works are likewise comprehensible. But lo, they shall now believe, because they see which heretofore could scarcely believe. Strong is the

---

23. 'Sweet Wood' or 'Swete Wood' is *Laurus Nobilis* or the Bay Tree, of which Nicholas Culpeper says: "Bay is a Tree of the Sun under Leo; it resisteth witchcraft very potently." [REC]

CAP. 3

influence of thy super-celestial power: and mighty is the force of that arm which overcometh all things. Let all power rest in thee, Amen.

Leave out the Bees of the 7 names of the 7 Kings, and 7 Princes, and place them in a Table divided 12 by 7. The 7 spaces being uppermost. And therein write in the upper line, the letters of the King with the letters of his Prince following next after his name. And so of the six other: and their Princes and read them on the right hand, from the upper part to the lowest. And thou shalt find then the composition of this Table. Therein they are all comprehended, saving certain letters, which are not to be put in here. By reasons THAT THE KINGS AND PRINCES DO SPRING FROM GOD: AND NOT GOD FROM THE KINGS AND PRINCES. Which excellence is comprehended and is also manifest in that third and fourth member. (**Dee:** fourth number). Round about the sides (of this square Table) is every letter of the 14 names of the 7 Kings and Princes. HEREAFTER SHALL YOU PERCEIVE THAT THE GLORY OF THIS TABLE SURMOUNTETH THE GLORY OF THE SUN. [11]

All things else that appertain unto it are already prescribed, by your former instruction.

IL, Dee: or – E

APRIL 29, 1583:

God is the beginning of all things, but not after one sort: nor to every one alike. But it is three manner of works with his name:

The One in respect of dignification.

The Second in respect of conciliation.

The Third in respect of an end and determined operation.

Now Sir, to what end would you wear your Character? etc. But

THE HEPTARCHIA MYSTICA

how do I teach? The Character is an instrument applicable only to dignification. BUT THERE IS NO DIGNIFICATION (Sir) but that which doth proceed and hath his perfect composition centrally in the square number of 3 and 4. The centre whereof and shall be equal to the greatest. Hereby you may gather, not only to what end the BLESSED CHARACTER (wherewith thou shall BE DIGNIFIED) is prepared: but also the nature of ALL OTHER CHARACTERS.

To the second

Dee:
Conciliation you mean?

IL:
The Table is an instrument of conciliation, and so are the other 7 CHARACTERS WHICH YOU CALL BY THE NAME OF TABLES: squared out into THE FORM OF ARMS: which are proper TO EVERY KING AND PRINCE — according to their order: Now to the last —

Dee:
As containing the end and determined operation?

IL:
It only consisteth in the mercy of God and the Characters of these books, etc.

Set down the Kings and their Princes in a Table, as thou knowest them, with their letters backward (excepting their bees) from the right hand to the left. Let Bobogel be the first and Bornogo his Prince, etc. (**Dee** – *Note*: here it may appear that 'Bvtmono is Prince to Bynepor and Blisdon Prince to King Bnaspol.)

CAP. 3

D. *Note*:
So on my Character or Lamyne of Dignification are all the names of the 7 Kings and of the 7 Princes, perfectly as in the great Table (called often Mensa foederis) the Bees, only being the first letter (common to them all) kept back in memory.
De Sigillo Æmeth: aliter vocato Sigillo Dei. (*Otherwise called the Sigil of God.*) [12]

MICHAEL:
I will show thee in the mighty hand and strength of God. What his mysteries are: the true circle of his eternity comprehending all virtue: the whole and sacred Trinity; Oh, holy be he, Oh holy be he, Oh holy be he. (**Dee** — Uriel answered, Amen.)

MICHAEL:
Now what wilt thou?

Dee:
I would full fayne proceed according to the matter in hand.

MICHAEL,
MARCH 19, 1582:
Divide this outward circle in 40 equal parts, whose greatest numbers are 4. See thou do it presently.

Dee:
I did so dividing it first into 4, and then every of them into 10.

Dee:
He called one, by name Semiel, one came in and kneeled down, and great fire came out of his mouth. Michael said: "*To him are the mysteries of these Tables known.*"

THE HEPTARCHIA MYSTICA

Michael said, Semiel (again) and by and by he answered: "*O God thou hast said and thou livest for ever: etc.*"

Semiel stood up and flaming fire came out of his mouth, and then he said as followeth:

SEMIEL:
Mighty Lord what wouldst thou with the Tables.

MICHAEL:
It is the will of God thou fetch them hither.

SEMIEL:
I am his Tables, behold, these are his Tables, lo where they are.

Dee:
There came in 40 white creatures, all in white silk long robes; and they like children. And all they falling on their knees said: "*Thou only art holy among the Highest: O God, thy name be blessed for ever.*"

Dee:
Michael stood up out of his chair: and by and by all his legs seemed to be like two pillars of brass: and he as high, as half way to heaven: and by and by his sword was all on fire: and he stroke or drew his sword over all these 40 their heads. The Earth quaked, and the 40 fell down. And Michael addressed Semiel with a thundering voice; and said: *Declare the mysteries of the Living God; our God: of One that liveth for ever.* (Michael 1582, March 19)

SEMIEL:
I am ready.

CAP. 3

(**Dee:** Then stepped forth one of the 40 from the rest: and opened his breast which was covered with silk, and there appeared a great

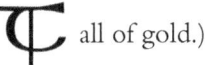 all of gold.)

MICHAEL:
Note the number.

Dee:
 Over the T stood the number of 4, in this fashion

Dee:
The 40 all cried, it liveth, and multiplieth for ever, blessed be his name.

Dee:
That creature did shut up his bosom and vanished away like a fire.

MICHAEL:
Place that in the first place: it is the name of God.

(**Dee:** Then there seemed a great clap of thunder to be: and so forth: and note that the whole Second Book is nothing else but the mysteries most marvellous of Sigillum Dei, otherwise called Sigillum Æmeth, whereof here I did but leave a little admonishment. *Note further:* almost all of the Third Book was of the 7 Ensigns of Creation, whereof mention was here before made.)

(**Dee:** The chair was brought in again: and I asked what it meant?)

THE HEPTARCHIA MYSTICA

URIEL:

This is a seat of perfection; from which things shall be showed unto thee, which THOU HAST LONG DESIRED.

(**Dee:** Then was a square Table brought into the stone, and I demanded what the Table betokened.)

URIEL:

A mystery not yet to be known. These two shall remain in the stone, to the sight of all undefiled creatures. You must use a FOUR SQUARE Table: two cubits square, whereupon must be set Sigillum Dei: (aliter divinitatis) (*otherwise of divinity*), etc.

This Seal is to be made of perfect wax.

This Seal must be 9 inches square (**D.** *Note*: or diameter) The roundness must be 27 inches, and somewhat more. The thickness of it must be an inch and a half quarter. And a figure of a Cross must be on the backside of it made thus:

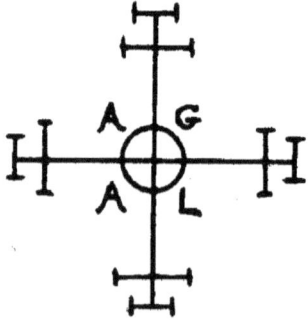

The Table is to be made of sweet wood: and of two cubits high with 4 feet, with 4 of the former seals under the 4 feet.

Dee:

Under the Table did seem to be laid red silk, two yards square. And over the Seal, did seem likewise red silk to lie four square,

CAP. 3

broader than the Table, hanging down with 4 knopps or tassels at the four corners thereof. Upon this uppermost red silk did seem the stone with the frame to be set: right over and upon the principal Seal: saving that the red silk was between the one and the other.

Dee:
There appeared the first Table covered with a cloth of silk changeable colour red and green with a white cloth under it, all hanging very low. [13]
NOVEMBER 21. A° 1582.

CAPUT 4

SOME NOTICE OF PECULIAR FORMS; AND ATTIRE; WHEREIN THE KINGS, PRINCES, AND MINISTERS HEPTARCHICAL APPEARED AND OF SOME OF THEIR ACTIONS AND GESTURES AT THEIR APPEARANCE, ETC.

KING CARMARA:

This King (being called first by Uriel) appeared as a man, very well proportioned, clad in a long purple robe, and with a triple Crown of Gold upon his head.

At his first coming he had 7 (like men) waiting on him: which afterward declared themselves to be the 7 Princes Heptarchical. Uriel delivered unto this King (at his first appearing) a rod, or straight little round staff of gold: divided into three equal distinctions whereof two were dark or black: and the third bright red. This rod he kept still in his hand. This King only was the orderer, or disposer of all the doctrines which I term Heptarchical, and first by calling the 7 Princes, and after that the 7 Kings: and by giving instructions for use and practice of the whole doctrine Heptarchical: for the first purpose and fruit thereof to be enjoyed by me: of the two other there was only mention made.

KING CARMARA said:

Ecce Signum Operis. (*Behold, the Sign of the Work.*)

CAP. 4

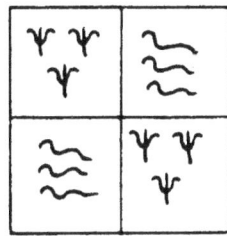

There appeared these two letters reversed and aversed on a white flag, and a woman standing by: whose arms did not appear: on the other side appeared the Arms of England. The flag old. [14]

PRINCE HAGONEL:

Note: All the Princes seemed to be men, and to have red robes, but this Prince, his robe was shorter than the others. All the Princes had circlets of gold on their heads, not crowns, nor coronets. This Prince held in the palm of his right hand as it had been a round ring with a prick in the midst: hanging also over his middle fingers which he affirmed to be his Seal and said the name of it to be Barees: and this it is: ⊙

All the Princes held up together Heptagon Stellar (as I term it) and it seemed to be of copper.

THE HEPTARCHIA MYSTICA

SUBJECTS AND SERVANTS TO PRINCE HAGONEL:
The Sons of men (**D.** Light) and their Sons are subject unto his commandment and are his servants.

7 Filii Lucis	I, Ih, Isr, Dmal, Heeoa, Beigia, Stimcul	In Sigillo Æmeth
7 Filii Filiorum	E, An, Ave, Liba, Rocle, Hagonel, Ilemese	

7 FILII LUCIS (7 SONS OF LIGHT):
A° 1582, March 21:

The 7 Filii Lucis appeared like 7 young men, all with bright countenance, white apparelled with white silk on their heads, pendant behind, with a wreath down to the ground all apparelled of one sort. Every one seemed to have a metalyn ball in his hand: the first of gold; the second of silver; the 3rd of copper; the 4th of tin; the 5th of iron; the 6th tossed between his two hands a round thing of quick-silver; the last had a ball of lead. The first had on his breast a round tablet of gold and on it written a great I, and the second on his golden tablet had his name also written: and every one orderly coming forth showed their names upon their golden tablets: at their departing they made curtsy, and mounted up to heavenward.

7 FILII FILIORUM (7 SONS OF SONS):

Appeared like 7 little children, like boys covered all with purple, with hanging sleeves, like priests' or scholars' gown-sleeves: their heads attired all after the former manner with purple silk. They had three-cornered tablets on their breasts: and the tablets seemed to be very green, and on them the letters of their names written. The first two letters made in one type,

CAP. 4

of E & L = E . They made reverences to Michael (who have called the first and these) and so mounted up to heavenward.

PRINCE HAGONEL,
HIS 42 MINISTERS:
At the call of King Carmara (in the second handling this Heptarchical doctrine), when he said: Venite Repetamus Opera Dei (*Come let us seek the works of God*): Appeared Prince Hagonel and after that upon the Globe his convex superficies appeared 42: who said: Parati sumus service Deo nostro (*We are ready to serve our God*). Each of these had somewhat in their hands and they stood in this order, and Hagonel seemed to embrace the company:

Six of these seemed more glorious than the rest and their coats longer and had circlets of gold about their heads, and hold in their hands perfect crowns of gold. The second six had three quarters of crowns in their hands. The third six have robes or clothes in their hands. All the rest seemed to have balls of gold

THE HEPTARCHIA MYSTICA

which they toss from one to another but at the catching, they seemed empty wind-balls, for they grip them closing their hands as if they were not solid, but empty like a blown bladder.

The first six made curtsy to Prince Hagonel, the second six made curtsy to the first, and the third to the second. And they all, and Prince Hagonel, made curtsy to King CARMARA. Each of these upon their place of standing made a Table, and every Table had but one letter. The first of the six did go away and in his Table appeared an O, and so of the rest: but note that the third six cowered down, and was loath to show their Tables, but at length did.

The third row went off lamenting: being commanded by their Prince: all parted in fire, falling into the Globe. The fifth row did sink into the Globe, every one in a sundry fire by himself.

The sixth fell with smoke down into the Globe.

```
O E S N G L E
A V Z N I L N
Y L L M A F S
N R S O G O O
N R R C P R N
L A B D G R E
```

KING CARMARA said: Remember how they stood, where they were secondly disposed unto thee. They stood first in six rows: and next they were turned into seven. I speak of the greater number and not of the less: in speaking the greater I have comprehended the lesser.

CAP. 4

Dee (*note*):
King CARMARA:
There are but 6 names that are in subjection unto the Princes: the first 7 next him are those which held the fair and beautiful crowns.

The first 7 are called by those names that thou seest OES (or OFS), etc:

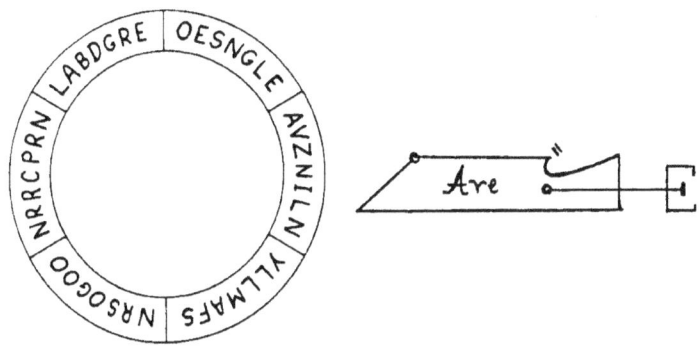

Dee. *Note:* This diversity of reckoning by 6 and by 7 I cannot yet well reconcile.

KING BOBOGEL:

Appeared in a black velvet coat: and his hose close round hose with velvet upperstocks: overlayed with gold lace: on his head a velvet hat-cap: with a black feather in it: with a cape hanging on one of his shoulders, his purse, hanging about his neck, and so put under his girdle at which hung a gilt rapier. His beard was long, he had pantafels and pynsons, and he said: I wear these robes, not in respect of myself, but of my government, etc. [15]

THE HEPTARCHIA MYSTICA

PRINCE BORNOGO:
Appeared in a red robe with a gold circlet on his head: he showed his Seal, and said: This it is:

MINISTERS 42:
Seven of the Ministers are apparelled like Bobogel the King, sagely and gravely: all the rest are almost ruffian or royster-like. Some are like to be men and women: for in the forepart they seemed women, and the back part men, by their apparel. And they were the last 7. They danced, leapt and kissed.

They came afterwards into a circle, the Sages and the rest: but the Sages stand all together. The first of the Sages lifted up his hand aloft and said: Faciamus secundum voluntatem Dei. Ille Deus poster est vere nobilis et aeternus. (*Let us perform according to God's wishes. He, our God, is truly noble and eternal.*)

He plucked up his right foot and under it appeared an L, and of the rest in like manner appeared their letters or names.

    1. The first 7 grow all together in a flame of fire, and so sunk down in the transparent fiery-Globe of the new world.
    2. The second 7 fell down like drops of metal.
    3. The third 7 clasp together and fall down in a thick smoke.
    4. The 4th seven join together and vanish like drops of water.
    5. The 5th seven fall down like a storm of hail.
    6. The last vanished away.

At another time they came (being called by King Carmara) all 42 bringing a round Table over their heads flat wise: and then they laid it down and stood about it: the letters being as before:

CAP. 4

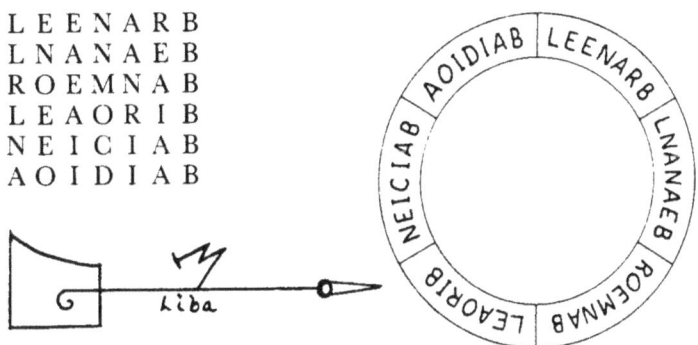

KING BABALEL:

Appeared with a crown of gold on his head: with a long robe white of colour. His left arm sleeve was very white and his right arm sleeve was black. He seemed to stand upon water. His name was written on his forehead: BABALEL.

PRINCE BEFAFES:

He appeared in a long red robe with a circlet of gold on his head. He had a golden girdle and on it written: BEFAFES.
He opened his bosom and appeared lame: and seemed to have feathers upon his robes.
His Seal or Character is this:

MINISTERS 42:

Of his 42 Ministers, the first 7 had circlets of gold on their heads, and the King BABALEL called BEFAFES saying: Veni

THE HEPTARCHIA MYSTICA

Princeps 7 Principum qui sunt Aquarum Principes. (*Come Prince of the seven Princes who are Princes of the Waters.*) Every one of the 42 had a letter on his forehead. They were 7 in a row and 6 downward. But of the first 7 the letters become to be between their feet: and the water seemeth continually to pass over these letters.

The first 7 take the water and throw it up, and it becometh clouds.

The second throw it up, and it becometh hail and snow, etc.

The 42 dive into the water, and so vanish away and BABALEL and BEFAFES also were suddenly gone.

Their names and characters appeared to be these which follow in the squares:

E I L O M F O
N E O T P T A
S A G A C I Y
O N E D P O N
N O O N M A N
E T E V L G L

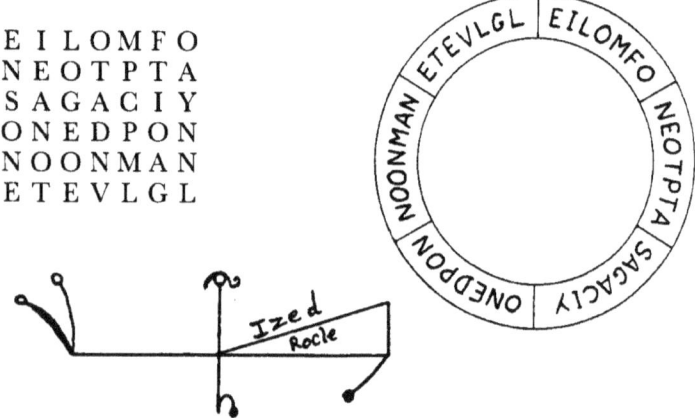

KING BYNEPOR:

He appeared as a King with his Prince next after him: and after the Prince 42 Ministers.

CAP. 4

PRINCE BVTMONO:

He appeared in a red robe with a gold circlet on his head. His Seal is this:

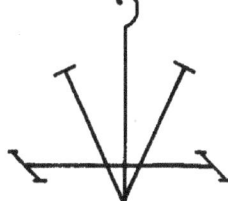

MINISTERS 42:

They appeared like ghosts and smoke without all form having every one of them a little glittering spark of fire in the midst of them.

The First 7 are red as blood.

The Second 7 not so red.

The Third 7 like whitish smoke. These [first three] had the sparks greater than the rest.

The Fourth, the Fifth, the Sixth are of divers colours. All had fire sparks in their middle.

Every spark had a letter in it as followeth:

B	B	A	R	N	F	L
B	B	A	I	G	A	O
B	B	A	L	P	A	E
B	B	A	N	I	F	G
B	B	O	S	N	I	A
B	B	A	S	N	O	D

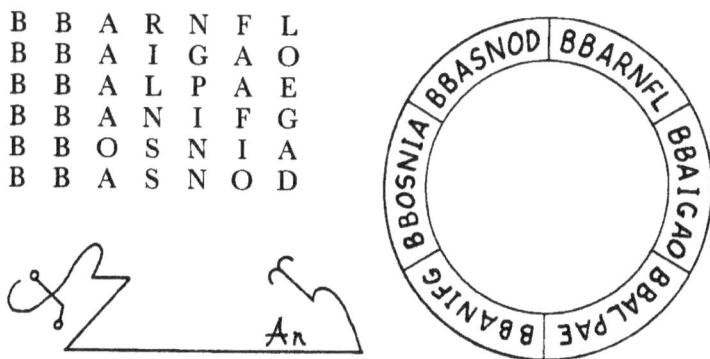

THE HEPTARCHIA MYSTICA

KING BNASPOL:
He appeared in a red robe, and a crown on his head. His Prince followed him, and after him his Ministers.

PRINCE BLISDON:
He appeared in a robe of many colours and on his head a circlet of gold.
His character or seal:

Dee:
Perhaps the red colour was most and so seemed generally to be red as the others their robes were.

MINISTERS 42:
The 42 seemed to stand about a little hill round. The hill was of clay. [16]

Behind these people seemed to stand an innumerable multitude of ugly people, afar off. Those which seem to stand about the little hill, seem to have in the palms of their hands letters in order as here appeareth. Those which stood afar off are spirits of perdition, which keep earth with her treasure for him, etc. [24]

E L G N S E B
N L I N Z V B
S F A M L L B
O O G O S R S
N R P C R R B
e r g d b a b

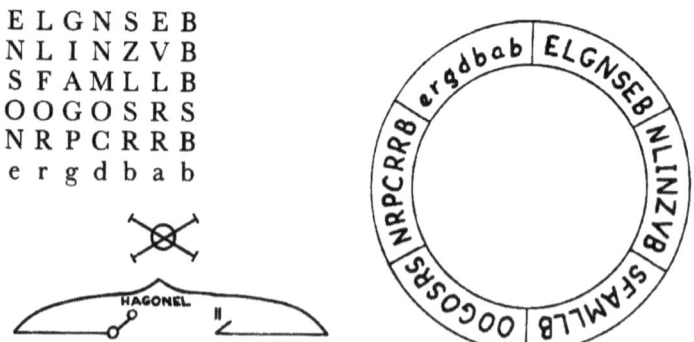

24. The following letters 'ergdbab' are in lower case in the manuscript

CAP. 4

KING BNAPSEN:

He appeared as a King with a crown on his head.

PRINCE BRORGES:

He appeared in his red apparel: and he opened his clothes and there did issue mighty and most terrible or ghastly Flames of Fire out of his sides: which no mortal eye could abide to look upon any long while. And in the marvellous raging fire did the word BRORGES appear, tossed to and fro in the very flames. His seal or character is this: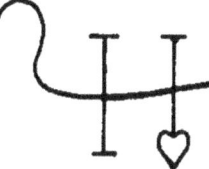

MINISTERS 42:

The 42 appear and holding a round Table, they toss it in the fiery flames.

Dee:

In the Table were the letters of their names as followeth:

B A N S S Z E
B Y A P A R E
B N A M G E N
B N V A G E S
B L B O P O O
B A B E P E N

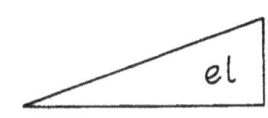

THE HEPTARCHIA MYSTICA

KING BALIGON:

He is the same mighty King, who is here first described by the name of CARMARA, and yet otherwise among the Angels called MARMARA, but that M is not to be expressed. Therefore he appeared in a long purple gown, and on his head a triple crown of gold, with a measuring rod of gold in his hand, divided into three equal parts: in the form of a very well proportioned man.

PRINCE BAGENOL:

He appeared not by that name yet. [17]

MINISTERS:

Note: The King himself is Governor over these. The 42 Ministers appeared like bright people. And besides them, all the air swarmed with creatures.

Their letters were on their foreheads.

They stood in a circle. They took their letters from their foreheads and set them in a circle:

A O A Y N N L
L B B N A A V
I O A E S P M
G G L P P S A
O E E O O E Z
N L L R L N A

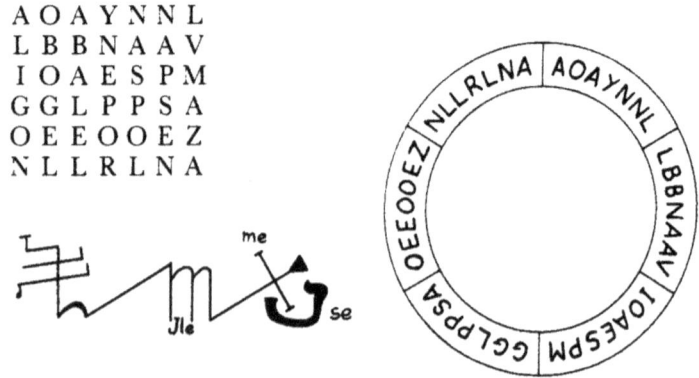

CAP. 4

KING BLVMAZA:
Dee, *Note*: He appeared not yet by that name.

PRINCES BRALGES:
He appeared in a red robe with a circlet on his head and he was the last of the 7 which hold the Heptagonon, all the rest being set down: who seemed now to extend their hands one towards another: as though they played, being now rid of their work.

MINISTERS:
The Powers under his subjection are invisible. They appeared like little white smokes without any form.
All the World seemed to be in brightness.
This is the Seal of his Government:

CAP. 5

ORATIO, AD DEUM, SINGULIS DIEBUS, TRIBUS VICIBUS, TER DICENDA.
(A PRAYER TO GOD TO BE RECITED THRICE DAILY.)

O Almighty, Æternal, the True and Living God: O King of Glory: O Lord of Hosts: O Thou, the Creator of Heaven and Earth, and of all things visible and invisible: now, (even now, at length) among others thy manifold mercies used and to be used, toward me, thy simple servant John Dee, I most humbly beseech thee, in this my present petition to have mercy upon me: to have pity upon me, to have compassion upon me: who, faithfully and sincerely, of long time, have sought among men, in Earth: and also by prayer, (full oft, and pitifully,) have made suit unto thy Divine Majesty for the obtaining of some convenient portion of True Knowledge and understanding of thy laws and ordenances, established in the natures and properties of thy creatures: by which knowledge, thy Divine Wisdom, Power and Goodness, (on thy creatures bestowed, and to them imparted) being to me made manifest, might abundantly instruct, furnish and allure me, (for the same), incessantly to pronounce thy praises, to render unto thee most hearty thanks, to advance thy true honour, and to win unto thy name some of thy due Majestical Glory, among all people, and for ever. And whereas it has pleased thee (O God) of thy infinite Goodness, by thy

CAP. 5

faithful and holy Spiritual Messangers, to deliver unto me long since (through the eye and ear of E.K.) an orderly form and manner of Exercise HEPTARCHICAL: how, to thy Honour and Glory, and the comfort of my own poor soul, and of others thy faithful servant, I may at all times, use very many of thy good Angels, their counsels and helps: according to the properties of such their functions and offices, as to them, by thy Divine Power, Wisdom and Goodness is assigned, and limited: (which orderly form, and manner of Exercise, until even now, I never found so urgent opportunity, and extreme necessity, to apply myself unto). Therefore, I, thy poor and simple servant, do most humbly, heartily, and faithfully beseech thy Divine Majesty, most lovingly and fatherly to favour and thy Divine Beck to further this my present industry and endeavour to Exercise myself, according to the aforesaid orderly form and manner: and now (at length, but not too late) for thy dearly beloved Son IESVS CHRIST his sake (O Heavenly Father) to grant also unto me, this blessing and portion of thy Heavenly Graces: that thou wilt forthwith enable me, make me apt, and acceptable (in body, Soul, and Spirit), to enjoy always the Holy and friendly conversation, with the sensible, plain, full and perfect help, (in word and deed) of thy Mighty, Wise and Good Spiritual Messagers and Ministers generally: and namely of Blessed Michael, Blessed Gabriel, Blessed Raphael and Blessed Uriel: and also, especially of all those, which do appertain unto the HEPTARCHICAL Mystery isagogically, (as yet) and very briefly unto me declared: under the method of Seven Mighty Kings; and their Seven faithful and Princely Ministers, with their subjects, and servants, to them belonging. And in thy great mercy, and grace, on me bestowed, and to me confirmed (O

THE HEPTARCHIA MYSTICA

Almighty God) thou shalt, (to the great comfort of thy faithful servants) approve, to thy very enemies and mine, the truth and certainty of thy manifold most merciful promises, heretofore made unto me: and that thou art the True and Almighty God, Creator of Heaven and Earth, (upon whom I do call: and in whom I do put my trust). And thy Ministers, to be the true and faithful Angels of Light: which have hitherto principally and according to thy Divine Providence dealt with us: and also I, thy poor and simple servant, shall then in and by thee be better able to serve thee, according to thy wellpleasing to thy honour and glory. Yea, even in these most miserable and lamentable days. Grant, oh grant, O our Heavenly Father, grant this (I pray thee), for thy only begotten Son IESVS CHRIST, his sake: *Amen. Amen. Amen.*

CAP. 6

BONORUM ANGELORU HEPTARCHICORUM. PICE, DEUOTÆQUE INVITATIONES.
(PIOUS AND DEVOUT INVOCATIONS OF THE GOOD ANGELS OF THE HEPTARCHIA.)

THE GENERAL AND COMMON EXORDIUM, AND CONCLUSION APPERTAINING TO THE 7 HEPTARCHICAL KINGS INVITING:
O puissant and right Noble King (N) and by what name else soever thou art called, or mayst truly and duly be called: to whose peculiar Government, Charge, Disposition, and Kingly Office doth appertain thee (N etc.)[25]

In the name of the King of Kings, the Lord of Hosts, the Almighty God, Creator of Heaven and earth, and of all things visible and invisible: O right Noble King (N), come now and appear, with thy Prince and his Ministers, and subjects, to my perfect and sensible eye judgement: in a godly and friendly manner, to my comfort and help, for the advancing of the Honour and Glory of our Almighty God by my service. As much as by the Wisdom and Power, in thy proper Kingly office and Government, I may be holpen and enabled unto: Amen.

COME, O right Noble King (N) I say, COME, Amen. Gloria Patri, etc.[26]

---

25. Insert here the office of the King being invoked as given in Cap. 7. 26. "Glory be to the father, to the Son, and to the Holy Ghost, as it was in the beginning, is now and ever shall be, world without end, Amen". [REC]

THE HEPTARCHIA MYSTICA

THE GENERAL AND COMMON EXORDIUM AND CONCLUSION APPERTAINING TO THE 7 HEPTARCHICAL PRINCES INVITING:

O noble Prince (N) and by what name else soever thou art called, or mayst truly and duly be called: to whose peculiar Government, Charge and Disposition, Office and Princely Dignity doth appertain thee (N etc.)[27]

In the name of Almighty God, the King of Kings, and for his honour and Glory to be advanced by my faithful service. I require thee, O Noble Prince (N) to come presently, and to show thyself to my perfect and sensible eye judgement, with thy Ministers servants and subjects, to my comfort and help, in Wisdom and Power according to the properties of thy noble office:

COME, O Noble Prince (N) I say, COME, Amen. Pater noster, etc.[28]

---

27. Insert here the office of the Prince being invoked as given in Cap. 7.
28. The Lord's Prayer [REC]

CAP. 7

SOME RECITAL AND CONTESTATIONS BY THE PECULIAR OFFICES, WORDS AND DEEDS OF THE 7 HEPTARCHICAL KINGS AND PRINCES, IN THEIR PECULIAR DAYS TO BE USED:

SONDAYE:
KING BOBOGEL:

The distributing, giving and bestowing of wisdom and science. The teaching of true philosophy, true understanding of all learning, grounded upon wisdom: with the excellencies in nature: and of many other great mysteries, marvellously available, and necessary to the advancing of the Glory of our God and Creator. And who said to me, (in respect of these mysteries attaining) Dee, Dee, Dee, at length, but not too late.[29]

Therefore, in the name etc. [This is the second and third paragraphs of the invocation to the King. REC]

PRINCE BORNOGO:

The altering of the corruption of nature into perfection: the knowledge of metals. And generally the Princely Ministering to the right Noble and Mighty King BOBOGEL, in his government of distributing, giving and bestowing of wisdom,

---

29. This is the section to be inserted in the invocation to the King. [REC]

THE HEPTARCHIA MYSTICA

science, true philosophy and true understanding of all learning grounded upon wisdom and of other very many his peculiar royal properties. And who sayst to me: "What thou desirest in me shall be fulfilled".[30]

Therefore, in the name etc. [This is the second and third paragraphs of the invocation to the Prince. REC]

MONDAYE:
KING CARMARA:

Who in this Heptarchical Doctrine, at Blessed Uriel his hand, didst receive the golden rod of government and measuring, and the chair of dignity and doctrine: and didst appear first to us, adorned with a triple diadem in a long purple robe. Who saidst to me at Mortlake: I minister the strength of GOD unto thee. Likewise, thou saidst: These mysteries hath God lastly, and of his great mercies, granted unto thee. Thou shalt be glutted, yea filled: yea, thou shalt swell and be puffed up with the perfect knowledge of God's mysteries, in his mercies.

And saidst: This Art is to THE FARTHER UNDERSTANDING OF ALL SCIENCES, THAT ARE PAST, PRESENT OR YET TO COME. And immediately, didst say unto me: Kings there are in Nature, with Nature, and above Nature. Thou art dignified. And saidst, concerning the use of these Tables: This is but the first step: neither thou shalt practise them in vain: and saidst thus generally of God's mercies and graces on me decreed and bestowed. Whatsoever thou shalt speak, do or work, shall be profitable and acceptable. And the end shall be good.

Therefore, in the name etc.

---

30. This is the section to be inserted in the invocation to the Prince. [REC]

CAP. 7

PRINCE HAGONEL:
To whose commandments the Sons of Men (D. Light) and their Sons are subject: and are thy servants. To whose power the Operation of the Earth is subject. Who art the first of the twelve: and whose seal is called Barees and this ⊙ it is. At whose commandment are the Kings, Noblemen and Princes of Nature. Who art Primus and Quartus Hagonel. Who by the Seven of the 7 (which are the Sons of Sempiternity) dost work marvels amongst the people of the Earth: and hast said to me, that I also by the same thy servant should work marvels. O Noble Hagonel, who art Minister to the triple crowned King CARMARA: and notwithstanding art Prince over these 42 Angels, whose names and characters are here presented:
   Therefore, in the name etc.

KING BLVMAZA: [Nothing written for BLVMAZA in the manuscript. – RT]

PRINCE BRALGES:
Who saidst: The creatures living in thy dominion are subject to thy own power. Whose subjects are invisible: and which (to my seer) appeared like little smokes without any form. Whose seal of government is this:

Who saidst: Behold I am come,
I will teach the names without numbers.
The creatures subject unto me shall be
known to you.
   Therefore, in the name etc.

THE HEPTARCHIA MYSTICA

TVESDAYE:
KING BABALEL:
Who art King of the Waters: mighty and wonderful in Waters. Whose power is in the bowels of the Waters. Whose royal person with thy Noble Prince BEFAFES and his 42 Ministers the triple crowned King CARMARA bad me use to the glory, praise and honour of him, which created you all to the laud and praise of his Majesty.

Therefore, in the name etc.

PRINCE BEFAFES:
Who art Prince of the Seas. Thy power is upon the Waters. Thou drowndedst Pharaoh and hast destroyed the wicked. Thy name was known to Moses. Thou livedst in Israel: who hast measured the waters, who wast with King Solomon, and also long after that with Scotus: but not known to him by thy true name: for he called thee Mares. [18] And since, thou wast with none: except, when thou preservest me (through the mercy of God) from the power of the wicked: and wast with me in extremity. Thou wast with me thoroughly. Who of the Egyptians hath been called OBELISON in respect of thy pleasant deliverance. And by that name to me known: and of me noted in record, to be noble and courteous OBELISON. Whose noble Ministers 42 are of very great power, dignity and authority. As some in the measuring of the motions of the Waters, and saltness of the Seas, in giving good success in battles reducing ships, and all manner of vessels that float upon the Seas. To some all the fishes and monsters of the Seas, yea, all that liveth therein are well known: and generally are the distributors of God's judgements upon the Waters that cover the Earth. Others do beautify Nature in her composition.

CAP 7.

The rest are distributors and deliverers of the treasures and unknown substances of the Seas. Thou O Noble Prince BEFAFES hadst me use thee in the name of God.

Therefore, in the name etc.

WEDDENSDAYE:
KING BNASPOL:
To whom the Earth with her bowels and secrets whatsoever are delivered: and hast said to me: Heretofore what thou art, there I may know. Thou art great but (as thou truly didst confess) he in whom thou art, is greater than thou.

Therefore, in the name etc.

PRINCE BLISDON:
Unto whom the Keys of the Mysteries of the Earth are delivered. Whose 42 Ministers are Angels that govern under thee. All which thy mighty King BNASPOL bad me use and affirmed that they are and shall be at my commandment.

Therefore, in the name etc.

THVRSDAYE:
KING BYNEPOR:
Upon the distribution and participation of whose exalted, especial and glorified power, resteth only and dependeth the general state and condition of all things. Whose sanctification, glory and renown, although it had beginning, yet can it not, neither shall it have ending. He that measureth said, and thou was the end of his workmanship. Thou art like him and of him: yet not as partaking or adherent, but distinct in one degree.

THE HEPTARCHIA MYSTICA

When he came, thou was magnified by his coming and art sanctified, world without end.

    Vita Suprema. (*The Highest Life.*)
    Vita Superior. (*The Higher Life.*)
    Vita Infima tuis sunt mensurata manibus. (*The Lowest Life is measured by your hands.*)

Notwithstanding thou art not of thyself: neither is thy power thine own: magnified by his name, thou art in all: and all hath some being by thee: yet thy power is nothing, in respect of his power, which hath sent thee. Thou beginnest new worlds, new people, new Kings and new knowledge of a new government. And hast said to me: Thou shalt work marvellous, marvellously by my workmanship in the highest.

    Therefore, in the name etc.

PRINCE BVTMONO:

Who art life and breath in living creatures. All things live by thee: the image of one excepted. All the kinds of beasts of the Earth dost thou endue with thy life. Thy seal is their glory. O God, thou art sanctified: and thou rejoicest. The living, the end and all beginning of all beasts, thou knowest and by sufferance thou disposeth them until thy time be run.

    Therefore, in the name etc.

FRYDAYE:
KING BALIGON:

Who canst distribute and bestow at pleasure, all and whatsoever can be wrought in aerial actions. Who hast the government of thyself perfectly, as a mystery known unto thyself. Thou didst advertise me of this stone, and holy receptacle: both needful

CAP. 7

to be had: and also didst direct me to the taking of it up: being presently and in a few minutes of time, brought to my sight (from the Secret of the Depth, where it was hid, in the uttermost part of the Roman possession) which Stone, thou warnedst me, no mortal hand but mine own should touch: and saidst unto me: Thou shalt prevail with it, with Kings, and with all the creatures of the world. Whose beauty (in virtue) shall be more worth, than the Kingdoms of the Earth. For the which purposes here rehearsed: and other partly, now to be exercised and enjoyed: and partly hereafter more abundantly (as the Lord God of Hosts shall dispose), and also because thou thyself art Governor of the 42 thy mighty, faithful and obedient Ministers:
   Therefore, in the name etc.

A BY-NOTE: Of the former SHEW STONE.
Blessed Uriel said to me at Mortlake A° **1583, MAY 5**, a meridie, circa horam 4 am as followeth:

URIEL:
Thy Character must have the names of the five Angels (written in the midst of Sigillum Æmeth) graven upon the other side, in a Circle: in the midst whereof, must the Stone be (which was also brought). Wherein thou shalt AT ALL TIMES behold (privately to thyself) the state of God's people through the whole Earth.

THE HEPTARCHIA MYSTICA

MARGINAL NOTE:
Vide Suidam in dictione Ephod.
Ubi de Adamante quo diversis datis signis responsa deo consequebatur.
Vide: Epiphanium de Lapidibus praetiosis Rationali isto. Vide scripturas de Urim et Thummim. Vide Libros receptos Trebonae, etc. Scriptum est in Lege (inquit Epiphanius) Visionem quae Mosi in Monte apperuit et Legem datam in gemma Sapphyro fuisse expressam. Aut Mizaldus Memorabilium centuria 4, numero 94.

(See Suidas on the word Ephod where [he writes of] the diamond in which, on the giving of various signs, the answers from God proceeded. [19]
See Epiphanius with the same argument on precious stones. [20]
See the scriptures on Urim and Thummim. [21]
See the books received at Třeboň.
It is written in the law (says Epiphanius) that the vision which appeared to Moses on the Mount and the law given was expressed in a sapphire or the Memorabilium of Mizaldus, cent. 4, no. 94.) [22]

PRINCE BAGENOL:
[Nothing written for BAGENOL in the manuscript – RT]

SATERDAYE:

KING BNAPSEN:
Who hast said to me that by thee I shall cast out the power of all wicked spirits: and that by thee I shall or may know the doings and practice of evil men, and more that may be spoken or uttered to man.

Therefore, in the name etc.

CAP. 7

PRINCE BRORGES:
Who, being the Prince, chief Minister and Governor under the right puissant King BNAPSEN didst (to my seer) appear in most terrible manner with fiery flaming streams,[23] and saidst:

Noui Ianuam Mortis. Et percussit
Gloria Dei Impiorum parietes.
(*I know the door of death. And the glory of God has shaken the walls of the ungodly.*)

Therefore, in the name etc.

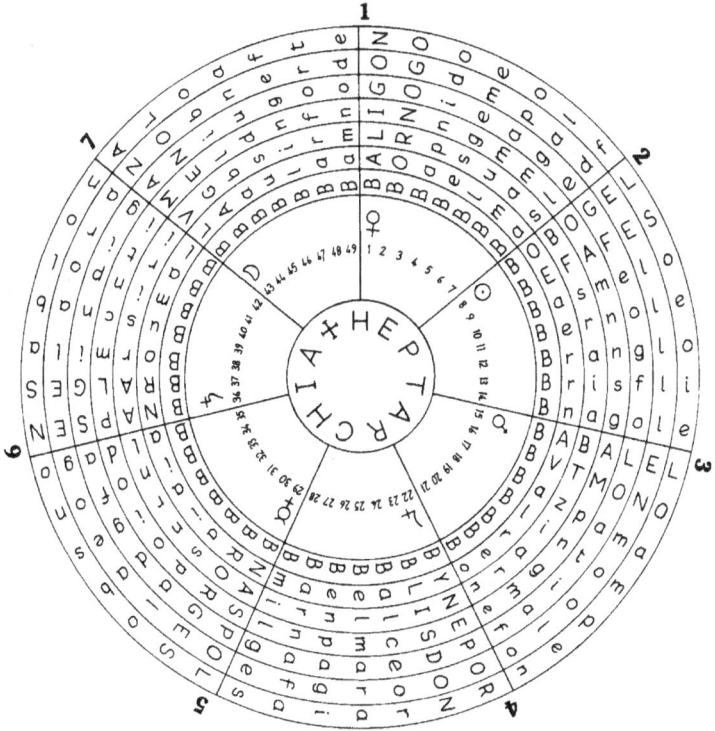

TABULA ANGELORUM BONORUM 49
The Table of 49 Good Angels [24]

APPENDIX A
ANALYTICAL NOTES

1. (a) A literal translation of the title *De Heptarchia Mystica* would be 'Concerning the Mystic Sevenfold Dominion' (ablative case following `de'). Alternative renderings are possible, i.e. (nominative case) 'The Mystic Sevenfold Dominion' or 'The Mystic Sevenfold Regimen'. The word 'Heptarchia' is low Latin, from the Greek *hepta* (seven) plus *arche* (rulership). English titles are normally in the nominative case.

(b) The prefatory quotation in Latin: '*In septenariis totus Mundus ... etc.*' is taken from the sixth book of the unfinished *Stromateis* ('Miscellanies') of Clement of Alexandria.

Titus Flavius Clemens, or Clement Alexandrine (c. 150 - 215 AD), a Christian theologian of the Alexandrian school, born probably in Athens of pagan parents, tried to reconcile Greek philosophy with the Mosaic Tradition of the Jews with considerable success. In the early third century A.D. he became one of the major intellectual leaders of the early Christian community.

THE HEPTARCHIA MYSTICA

In *Stromateis* he sets down his philosophical ideas in a series of unsystematic (Gnostic) notes.

2. (a) The ring referred to is not described in detail in the present text. However, a representation of its design is recorded in John Dee's *Mysteriorum Liber Primus: Mortlaci* (*First Book of the Mysteries: Mortlake*, British Library Sloane MS 3188).

On Wednesday March 14, 1582, the Archangel Michael

John Dee's drawing of the Ring

reveals the form of the ring to Dee – via Kelley – who describes it in the following manner:

Dee: Then he (Michael) laid the ring upon the table. It seemed to be a ring of gold: with a seal engraved on it, and had a round thing in the middle of the seal, and a thing like a V, through the top of the circle: and an L, in the bottom: and a

APPENDIX A

bar clear through it. And had these four letters in it, P E L E...

PELE is an Angelic name meaning: '*He who workest wonders*', and according to a marginal note in the manuscript, Dee recognized the name from John Reuchlin's work *De Verbo Mirifico*, a copy of which is included in his library catalogue and made the following note:

'*Vide Reuchlin, Librum de virbo mirico, de nom PELE*'.

(b) With regard to the choice of Lamyne, a certain amount of controversy exists. The first example revealed in the Spiritual Diaries is that which follows *Mysteriorum Liber Primus,* March 10, 1582:

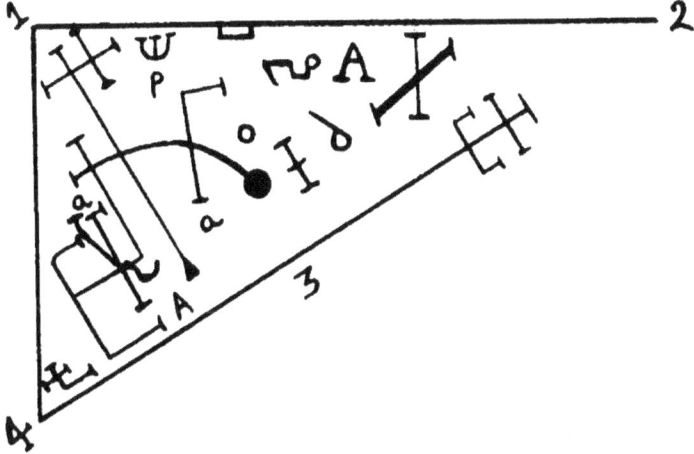

Two marginal notes cast doubt on the validity of this character (said to have originated from the Archangel Uriel):

(i) 'An illuding spirit straight away introduced himself and this character as may appear *Quinti Libri Mysteriorm Appendix* (*Appendix to the Fifth Book of the Mysteries*), where the character is described exactly.'

THE HEPTARCHIA MYSTICA

(ii) 'This was not the True Uriel as may appear A° 1583: May 5.'

In the *Quinti Libri Mysteriorm Appendix*, Dee is told by the Angel IL that the first revealed Lamyne was 'false and divilish', and therefore not to be employed. Another Lamyne is then revealed by the Angel, first in Roman letters, and later to be converted into the characters of the Angelic Alphabet. Both designs, false and true, were held to contain a 'token' of Dee's name, 'a certain shadow of Delta', but it seems that Dee never understood how this could be. As an explanation, the Angel refers to the characters in the corners of the Lamyne, but unless some form of cypher is involved, it is difficult to see how the letters represent Dee's name.

The True Lamyne (*first form: Roman letters*):

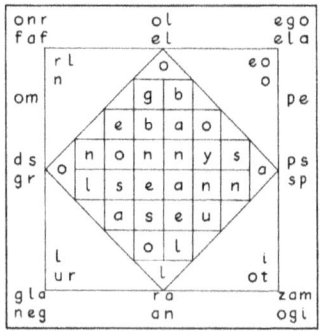

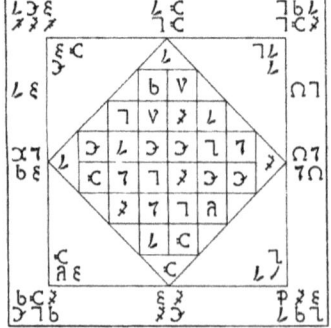

The True Lamyne (*second form: Angelic letters*):

APPENDIX A

Dee is instructed to draw the above figure on paper four inches square. In use it was to be hung round the neck as a defence against evil spirits.

3.(a) Sigillum Æmeth: Dee's principal seal consisted of a wax disc 9 inches in diameter and 1.25 inches in thickness, upon which were described certain characters and numbers: a heptagon, a heptagram, and a pentagram, together with various Angelic names and seals. The seal's design was transmitted to Dee via a series of spiritual communications that took place in March 1582 (*Mysteriorum Liber Secundus - The Second Book of the Mysteries*).

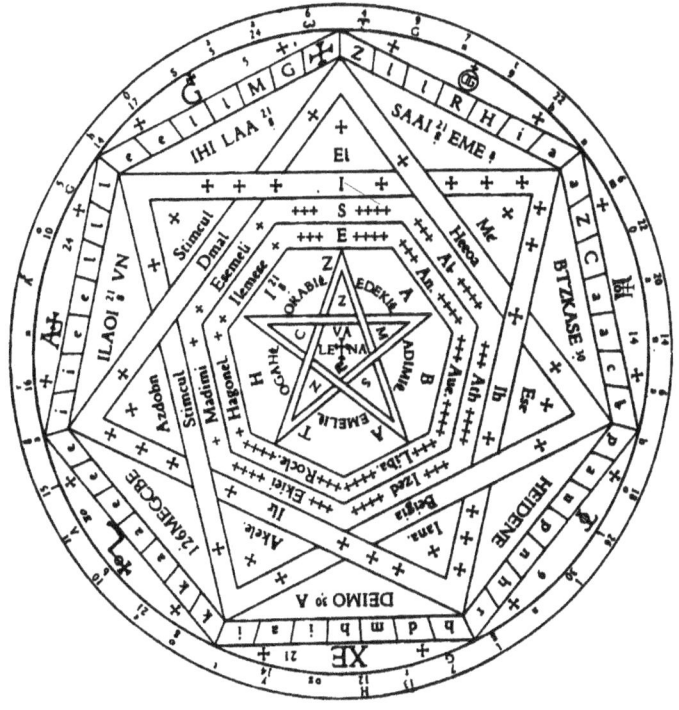

Sigillum Æmeth

THE HEPTARCHIA MYSTICA

In use, the seal supported the shew-stone, or crystal, four smaller versions being placed under the four legs of the Holy Table, protected from possible damage by wooden cases.

The major version of Sigillum Æmeth, and two of the smaller seals, can be seen to this day in the collection of the British Museum. It seems that they were donated to the Museum, along with the books from the Cottonian Library, as indicated in the following extract from *The Proceedings of the Society of Antiquaries of London* XXI (1906-7) by Ormonde J. Dalton:

> *The curious wax discs engraved with magical figures and names probably came into the British Museum with the books of the Cottonian Library, for among these books were two volumes of MS diaries written by Dr John Dee (1527-1608), the celebrated mathematician and astrologer; and Meric Casaubon relates that Dee's 'Holy Table', with which these discs have the closest connection, was in his time preserved in the library of Sir Thomas Cotton.*

The Hebrew word Æmeth (EMETH = truth) is the word of power that is said to have been employed by Rabbi Judah ben Bazalel Loew (1512/1526 - 1609) to animate the mysterious Golem of Prague.[31]

On his drawing of the seal to be found in BL Sloane MS 3188, Folio 30, Dee adds the Latin words '*nuncupatum Dei*' (the Name of God), indicating the level on which he regarded the symbol.

---

31. The word of power (the *shem* in Hebrew), *EMET*, was written on the forehead of the inanimate clay creature to bring it to life or on a piece of parchment placed in its mouth. To deactivate the golem, the *shem* was removed or the first letter (aleph) of *EMET* on the forehead erased. The word now reads *MET* meaning 'death', turning the golem to dust.[REC]

APPENDIX A

Statue of the Rabbi Loew at the New City Hall (Nová radnice), Prague. (Photograph© R.E. Cousins)

On the reverse side of the Sigillum Æmeth, we find the well-known magical word of power AGLA, inscribed about an equal-armed cross. The word is formed from a Qabalistic method of notation called Notariqon, where the initial letters of a sentence are taken to form a word. Thus AGLA = Ateh Gebor Le-Olahm Adonai = Thou art mighty forever, O Lord.

THE HEPTARCHIA MYSTICA

(b) John Dee possessed several crystals and scrying mirrors and refers to them variously throughout the Spiritual Diaries. [Dee mentions three stones in the course of the actions. During the first action recorded in *Mysteriorum Liber Primus* (with Barnabus Saul on 22 December 1581) a 'great Chrystaline Globe' was used.[32] During the same action, Dee produced a second crystal described as the 'stone in the frame' which was later employed during the initial action with Kelley (then known as Talbot) on 10 March 1582. - AT]

There are two examples of Dee's scrying equipment displayed in the British Museum: a black obsidian mirror of Aztec origin,[33] and a small but perfect quartz crystal. The latter of these could be the 'stone in the frame', speculum or 'shew-stone' intended for the Heptarchical workings.

The 'stone in the frame' appears to have been used in subsequent actions until 21 November 1582, when an angel provided Dee with a third stone, as recorded in *Quartus Liber Mysteriorum*. A crude marginal drawing in the MS indicates that in use, the crystal was also set in a gold frame, surmounted by what looks like a Calvary Cross. Dee describes the event in the following words:

Dee: E.K. (Edward Kelley) looked toward my west wyndow, and saw there, first uppon the mats by my bokes a thing (to his thinking) as bigg as an egg: most bright, clere and glorious, and an Angel of the heyht of a little chylde holding up the same thing in his hand toward me: and that Angel had a fyrey sword in his hand, etc.

H [the Angel Hagenol]: *Go toward it; and take it up.*

---

32. The 'great Chrystaline Globe' is not mentioned again, so may have belonged to Barnabus Saul. [AT] 33. Although supposedly belonging to Dee, there is nothing matching its description in his diaries or any evidence that such a mirror was used for scrying. [AT]

APPENDIX A

Dee: *I went toward the place, which EK pointed to: and tyll I cam within two fote of it, I saw nothing, and then I saw like a shaddow on the ground or matts hard by my bokes under the west wyndow. The shaddow was rowndysh,, and less than the palm of my hand. I put my hand down uppon it, and felt a thing cold and hard: which (taking up) I perceyved to be the Stone before mentioned.*
H: *Kepe it sincerely.*

[The crystal on display in the British Museum cannot be the stone delivered by the angel, as Dee described it as being 'half an inch thik', thereby implying it was flat rather than spherical. [34] Both this and the original 'stone in a frame' (which could be the crystal exhibited in the Museum) appear to have been used interchangeably afterwards. Dee evidently took them to Europe, as references are made to both stones being removed from their frames during an action in Prague on 10 April 1586 and both being used simultaneously on 24 April 1587. - AT]

A note on the obsidian mirrors can be found on page 383 of the *Proceedings of the Society of Antiquaries* (O. M. Dalton, 1907):

. . . the best-known mirror is a flat piece of polished obsidian, evidently one of the mirrors used for toilet purposes by the ancient Mexicans.[35] *This mirror, which is in a leather case, was in the collection of Horace Walpole, and sold at the Strawberry Hill sale. It has changed hands a great many times, and when last put up*

---

34. After Dee died in 1609, his friend John Pontois inherited some of Dee's books and equipment including the Holy Table. Thomas Hawes , a local grocer, saw at Pontois's house in or near Bishopgate Street, a 'certain round flat stone like Christall which Pountis said was a stone which an Angell brought to doctor dye wherein he did worke and know many strange things...'. (*John Dee's Library Catalogue*, ed. Julian Roberts & Andrew G. Watson . London: The Bibliographical Society, 1990, p. 61) [AT]   35. It is possible that the obsidian mirror belonged to Dee, as he collected unusual artefacts. [AT]

THE HEPTARCHIA MYSTICA

for auction passed into the hands of Prince Alexis Soltykoff,[36] in whose possession it is still supposed to be. Another mirror, also of Mexican obsidian, and said to have belonged to Dr Dee, was sold at the Jeffrey Whitehead sale at Sotheby's in March 1906.

4. The tables upon which the feet of the operator are to be placed during the Heptarchical Workings are almost certainly those given in two forms at the end of each section of Chapter 4 of the main text. Each table contains 42 letters (being the names of the 42 Angelic Ministers), which are extracted by a laboriously complex method from the *Tabula Angelorum Bonorum 49* (Table of the 49 Good Angels). Of the two forms given (a 7 x 6 square and a circular formation), Dee indicates in his notes in *Quartus Liber Mysteriorum* (*The Fourth Book of the Mysteries*) that the circular table is to be employed in each case: 'Note the Circle upon the ground: vide ante 3 folio, of my feet placed upon these Tables: ergo they should seem to be on the ground.'

The seal of the appropriate Prince is then placed on top of the 42-fold table upon which the operator stands. Thus the circular form of the table: LEENARB, LNANAEB, ROEMNAB, LEAORIB etc. (second table 42 Ministers of Bornogo) would be overlaid by the seal of BORNOGO, etc.

5. Prince Hagonel's seal, known as Barees, is the planetary symbol of the Sun and the alchemical symbol for gold ☉. In a later section of *Liber Mysterorium Quartus* the symbol is recorded in conjunction

---

36. Prince Aleksei Demetrievich Saltykov or Soltykoff (1806 – 1859) was a Russian artist and traveller, known for his sketches of Indian life. The mirror was sold to picture frame manufacturer and fine art dealer Robert J. Stannard (1854-1907), before being purchased by the British Museum in 1966 from his son, the Revd. Bishop Robert W.Stannard (1895-1986). [REC]

APPENDIX A

with a Calvary Cross: ♀ followed by Dee's note: 'It should seem that this character should be only a circle and a prick fol. 6.6. I have forgotten how I came by the Cross annexed to it.'

6. *Mensafaderis* (Mensa Faederis): in English, 'League Table' or 'Table of Covenant'. Dee's Holy Table or Table of Practice upon which was set Sigillum Æmeth and the shew-stone. In his *The Life of John Dee* Thomas Smith writes:

> To this Table appertained a peculiar sacred, as it is called, Apparatus, that is to say, a coverlet, a white linen cloth spread over it, a desk, a candle-stick, a wax candle burning at the time of the Operation, a shrine in which red Crosses were interwoven all of which were kept, as is the custom, in the Oratory ... .

After Dee's death, the table passed into the library of Sir Thomas Cotton, along with a portion of the Spiritual Diaries and other items. In 1731 the Cottonian Library, then in Ashburnham House, was severely damaged by fire, and in 1753 its contents were removed to the British Museum. The whereabouts of the Holy Table are to this day unknown, and it is perhaps not unlikely to have been totally destroyed in the fire of 1731.

An engraving of the table was published by Dr Meric Casaubon in his 1659 edition of Dee's Spiritual Diaries (Books 6-18) entitled: *A True and Faithful Relation of What passed for many Years Between Dr John Dee and Some Spirits*. In the Preface of his *True and Relation*, Casaubon mentions that this engraving was taken from a brass cut he caused to be made from the original preserved in the library.

When one compares Casaubon's printed representation of the Holy Table with the drawing of the same given in *Quinti*

THE HEPTARCHIA MYSTICA

Libri Mysteriorum Appendix (the only diagram of the table given in the Spiritual Diaries), the fact emerges that Casaubon's rendering is quite plainly in error.[37] The letters that border the top and bottom edges of the table are obviously written backwards, while those that make up the left and right hand borders are transposed. In addition to these errors the 4 x 3 square that takes up the centre is also given in a reversed order. Detailed notes given in *Mysteriorum Libri Quinque* leave us in no doubt of the intended design of the table, and I am able to state with absolute certainty that Dee's drawing represents the correct form.

It should also be stated that, as all subsequently published renderings of the table – including the version printed in Crowley's *Equinox (VII)*, and those of various contemporary American organizations – have followed Casaubon, the situation has remained unrectified until the publication of the present volume.

From the above statement two questions clearly arise. Firstly, how could Casaubon's engraver have executed such a strangely orientated rendering of the design? Secondly, why have the 'authorities' on Dee's magical writings not discovered this mistake during the passage of the last three hundred and thirty years or so?

As a tentative answer to the first question, I am informed by an expert in early printing techniques that such mistakes were once fairly commonplace, owing to the methods then employed in the art of plate-making. When one considers the

---

37. Casaubon's engraving of Kelley's *Vision of the Four Castles* in *True and Faithful Relations* is also wrong. The colours of the four cloths attributed to the directions have been reversed, showing east as green (instead of red), west as red (instead of green), north as white (instead of black) and south as black (instead of white). All are correct in Dee's original diagram, indicating the engraver made errors. [AT]

APPENDIX A

upside-down sigils and imperfect magic squares of Barrett's *Magus*, this might well be the case.

The second question has, perhaps, several possible solutions. Occultists have long adhered to a tradition of imitating the mistakes of venerable predecessors, placing far too much reliance on the printed word, and rarely seeking verification of the facts through close examination of source material. One has only to consider the gross inaccuracies of the Golden Dawn system, and the travesties published by Aleister Crowley, to realize the validity of this point.[38]

Another factor that has perhaps helped to obscure the true interpretation of Dee's table is the inability of the normal mind to work simultaneously in two entirely different symbol systems. Casaubon's version of the Holy Table employs the somewhat alien characters of the Angelic Alphabet throughout, while Dee's diagram consists of Roman letters, with the Angelic characters to be included in the central square referred to by name only: Gisg, Gon, Med, Van, etc. Dee's diagram is therefore the prototype of what was finally rendered into the Angelic counterpart. In addition, various easily disregarded marginal corrections to the structural notes are to be found throughout the relevant text.

The letters that were to be included along the edges and within the central square of the table were obtained in the following manner. First Dee is instructed to make a square 7 x 12 and to write within it the fourteen names of the Heptarchical Kings and Princes backwards (i.e. right to left), in

---

38. Some scholars disagree. For example, Donald Tyson in *Enochian Magic for Beginners* (1997) writes '... the plate in Casaubon is probably a correct representation of Dee's Table of Practice. The artist ... seems to have done a fairly accurate job. Why should he make the glaring mistake of inverting everything from left to right ... especially when the Ensigns of Creation are not inverted, but occupy their correct positions?' (p. 69-71) [REC]

THE HEPTARCHIA MYSTICA

each case omitting the initial letter 'B'. Reading the letters of the square downwards from right to left yields the order of the letters read in a clockwise direction from the top right-hand corner of the table. (In order to achieve this, the top line of the table should be transferred to the bottom – [RT])

```
l o n e g a n o g i l a
o g o n r o l e g o b o
s e f a f e l e l a b a
o n o m t u r o p e n y
n o d s i l l o p s a n
s e g r o r n e s p a n
s e g l a r a z a m u l
```

To obtain the letters to be included in the central square (3x4), Dee is instructed to write the following by Uriel:

```
o o e
l r l
r l u
o i t
```

(The reversed and inverted letters of the central square).
Then: 'rather thus:'

```
t i o
u l r
l r l
e o o
```

(The correct form of the Square).

Dee's *note*: So they would seem to have been meant in the figure of the Table of Practice before described.

APPENDIX A

Uriel explains that these letters are obtained from a 7 x 12 table following the order of *Tabula Collecta* (the Table of the 49 Good Angels; see further note).

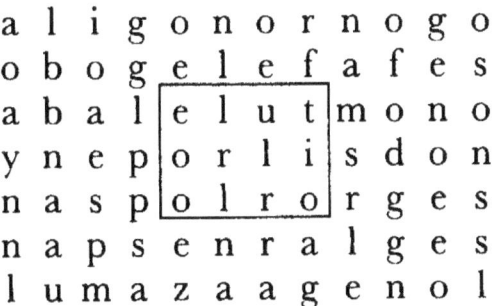

Once more omitting the Bs, but this time written from left to right. (Dee also lists the names of the Angelic equivalents of these letters against the various parts of the table: in front, to the right, to the left, and towards the breast.)

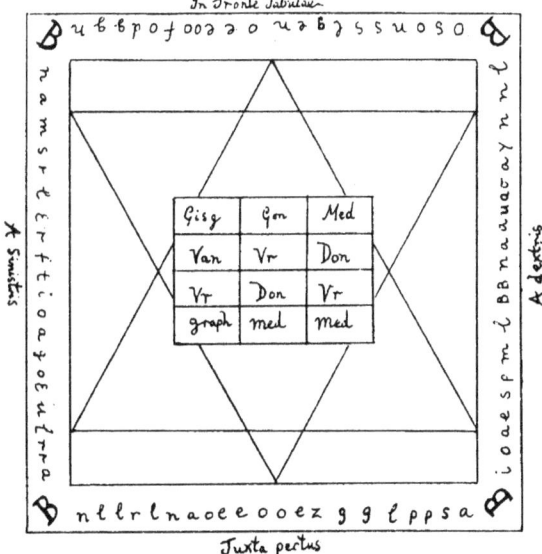

Dee's diagram of the Holy Table as given in *Quinti Libri Mysteriorum Appendix*.

THE HEPTARCHIA MYSTICA

Note: 'A great 'B' is to be made at each corner'.

Dee is instructed to render the letters into the characters of the Angelic Alphabet.

The Dimensions of the Table were two cubits square – i.e., 36 to 40 inches square – and two cubits high, having a leg at each corner. It was to be made of sweet wood, probably cedar, rosewood or pine.[39]

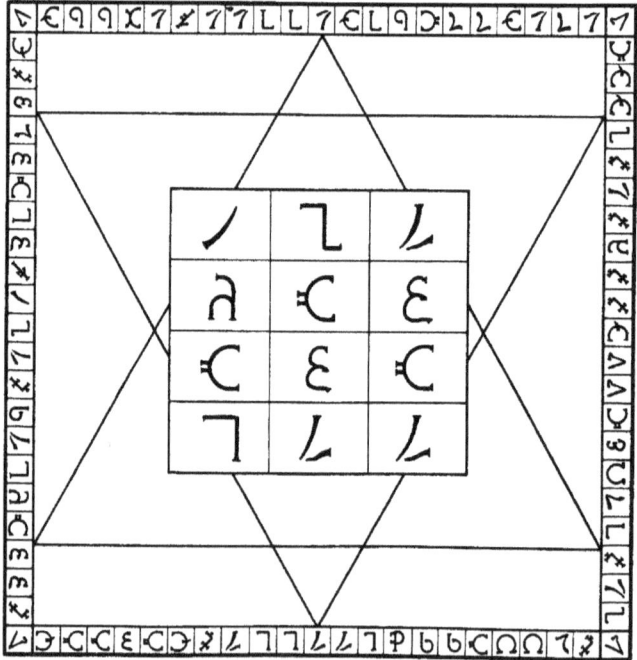

The Final Form of the Holy Table

---

39. As previously noted, 'Sweet Wood' or 'Swete Wood' is *Laurus Nobilis* or the Bay Tree, of which Nicholas Culpeper says: " Bay is a Tree of the Sun under Leo; it resisteth witchcraft very potently." [REC]

APPENDIX A

CHARACTER	VALUE	NAME	CHARACTER	VALUE	NAME	CHARACTER	VALUE	NAME
✗	A	Un	ᙏ	H	Na	Ⅱ	Q	Ger
V	B	Pa	ᒐ	I,Y	Gon	Ɛ	R	Don
ß	C,K	Veh	⊂	L	Ur	⌐	S	Fam
⊃⊂	D	Gal	Ȝ	M	Tal	✓	T	Gisg
ᒣ	E	Graph	Ȝ	N	Drux	ᕍ	U,V	Van
✗	F	Or	L	O	Med	Γ	X	Pal
ხ	G,J	Ged	Ω	P	Mals	ᛈ	Z	Ceph

The Angelic Alphabet

7. In use the Holy Table was to be set up in the following manner. First, the table was placed upon four smaller versions of Sigillum Æmeth which were protected by wooden cases. Then major version of Sigillum Æmeth was placed in the centre of the table and surrounded by seven tablets or tables made from purified tin (see note 9). The whole table was then covered with a drape of red cloth shot with green, which hung down the sides of the table with a tassel at each corner. On the top of the silken cloth – exactly over the Sigillum Æmeth stood the crystal, or shew-stone, within its golden frame.

Dee also notes in his first book that red silk 'two yards square' was also to be laid under the table; but whether this was to be laid over or under the four lesser seals is unclear. A crude diagram of the table without the table-cloths can be found in *Mysteriorum Liber Primus*.

With regard to the colouring of the table, very little is revealed, apart from the instruction that the characters written along the edges were to be rendered in yellow ('made perfect oil, used in the church').[40]

THE HEPTARCHIA MYSTICA

8. See Note 2(b)

9. The seven tablets or tables referred to are described in the Diaries as 'Arms' or 'The Ensigns of Creation'. They were obtained clairvoyantly during a series of operations which were carried out towards the end of April 1582. The Angel instructs Dee to make the tablets from purified tin, or to paint them on the table; which method was adopted is uncertain. A note in the *Quinti Libri Mysteriorum Appendix* explains that the tablets are 'proper to every King and Prince in their order'. The order in which the tablets were received is as follows:

Numerus Primus (The First Number)

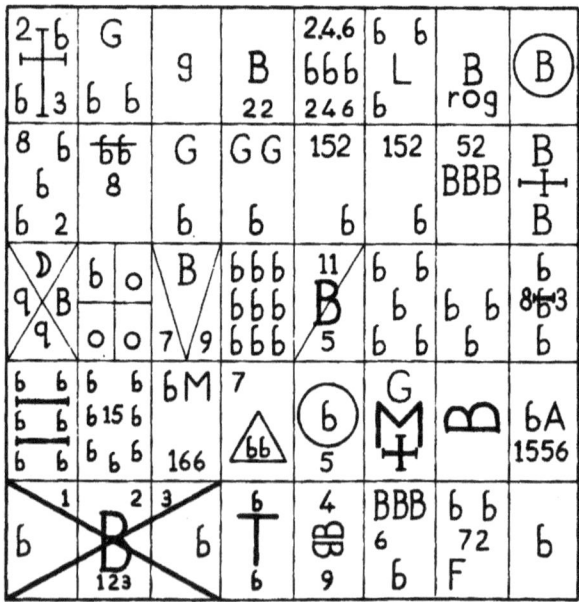

40. The yellow oil refers to characters found on the first form of the table that were later declared demonic. No other instructions were given by the angels regarding the colouring. It seems to have been left up to Dee. [AT]

APPENDIX A

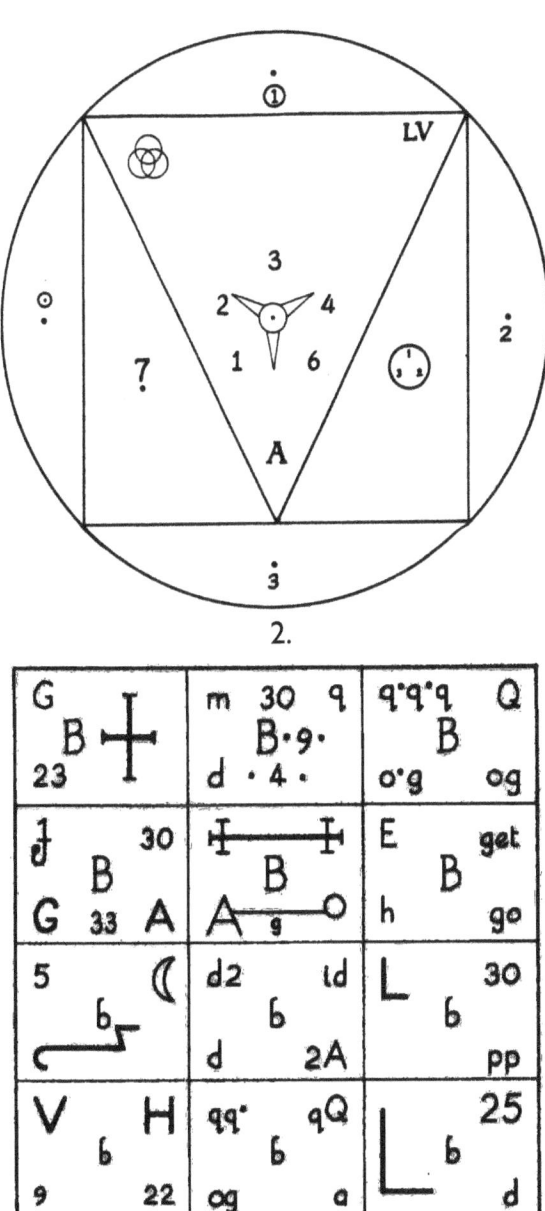

2.

3.

THE HEPTARCHIA MYSTICA

2 bb 2	bb ▽	537 bbb	b B G 11	T 13 bbb	b 9
V·2 B	o 4 B B	B 14 a	bbb P·3·	b G O	bb C:V 3
8 e b	Q·o 7 b b	∽∽ 5	q q b 3	q·9 B	L b· 8
go·30 B	9·3 bb	q q 5 ·b·b·	d┬ b┴A	7·2 b·B	B B ·∧· 8 3

4.

g D 2 g	B⧸⧹ l⧸l ⧸30	B B 8 2	B ♀ 22	B·o P d 30	L o B·q q·29	B ┼ 8 2	⧸9 6 B
o P B 9 8	┼ 9 ⌒ B	bb 2· 8·G	bb 9 E	b 3 Q	bbb 9 Q	b ii Q	B B 1 2 T
B B 68	M 2 bb	M 5 b	M bb b20	M 6·89 F	d B 17	┼ A 6 3	B⧸ B⧹B 2 H
M b gg L	b 6 ┼ 4 b	9 b ┼ 1 b	bb T 9·6	6 B 2 4	I B 38	N B 9	b b 4 b

5.

APPENDIX A

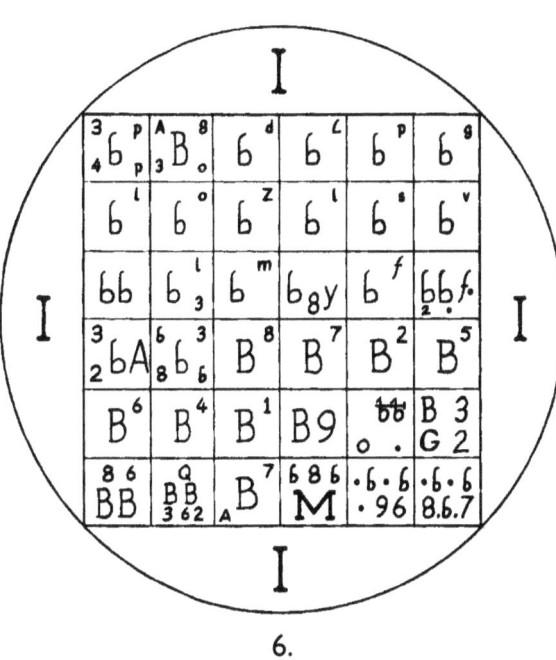

6.

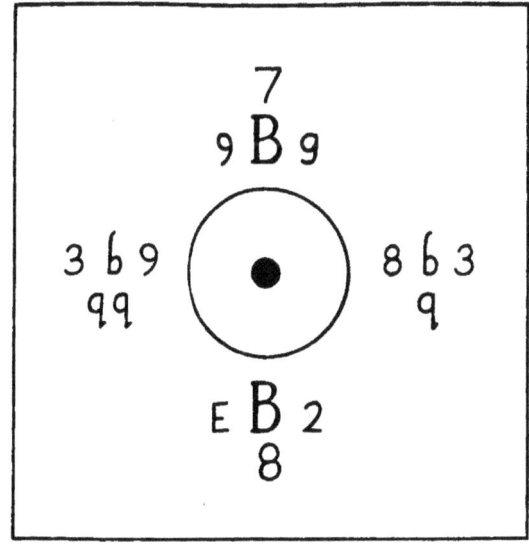

7.

THE HEPTARCHIA MYSTICA

In use the seven tablets were placed or painted upon the Holy Table in the following manner: (Note: Seven inches from the border of the table. Numbers indicate the order of the tablets given above).

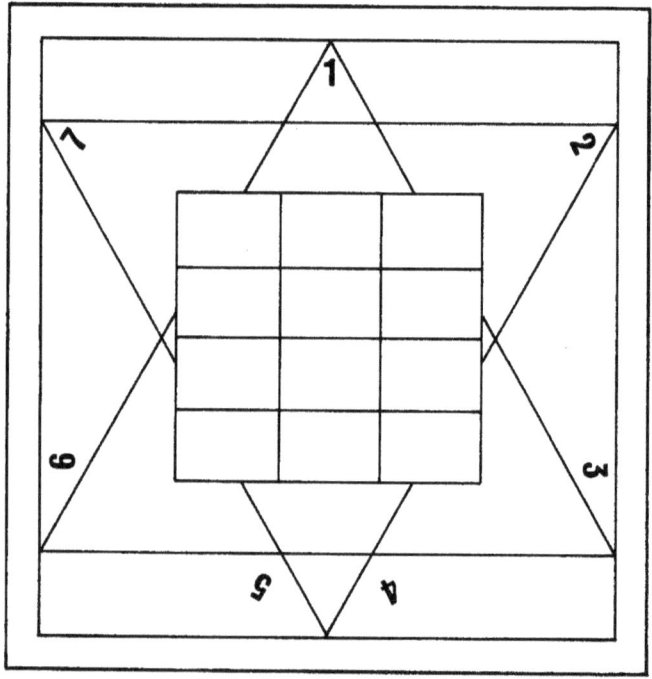

10. The tables to be held in the hand during the operation are to be painted on sweet wood. According to a marginal diagram in the *Quinti Libri Mysteriorum Appendix*, they take the form of three concentric circles. The central circle contains the sigil of the King, the second (middle) circle contains his name, and the third (outer) circle contains letters, some backward, some forward, obtained we are told from 'the Great Globe'.

APPENDIX A

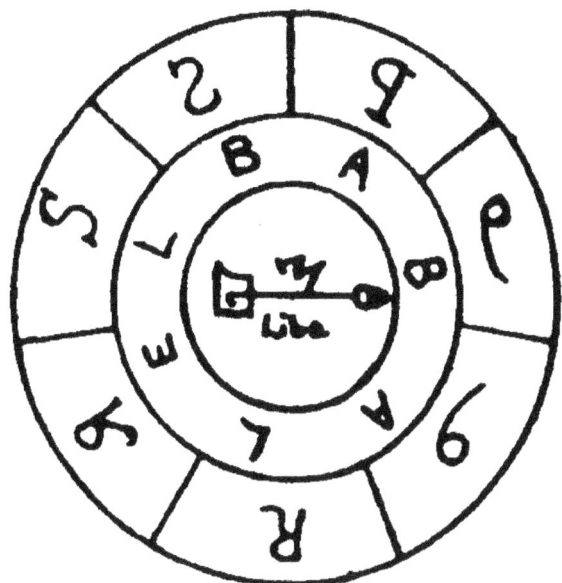

Dee's Marginal Diagram

It is uncertain what is intended by this last remark, as nothing in the Diaries seems to correspond to this device. Perhaps Dee refers to something revealed only in the crystal, or the relevant notes have not come down to us (see Introduction).

11. See note 6.

12. See note 2(b).

13. The white cloth corresponds to the visionary table employed by the Angels, and not to the Holy Table of Practice.

14. A vision of a strange flag is revealed to Kelley in the Action which opens the *Quartus Liber Mysteriorum*. A crude diagram

THE HEPTARCHIA MYSTICA

shows a woman and the reversed letters 'C B' on a white background. The other side of the flag contains the Royal Arms of England as employed from 1400-1603. Two quarters of the flag each contain three representations of the fleur-de-lis (representing France), and two quarters three lions passant guardant (for England).

15. *Pantafes*: a kind of high-heeled overshoe worn to raise the ordinary shoes out of mud and wet, secured to the foot by a leather loop. *Pynsono*: a thin shoe or slipper (a pump) to be worn with pantafes. Obsolete soon after 1600. No description known.

16. The following sketch of the hill and 42 Ministers is given in *Liber Mysteriorum Quintus*:

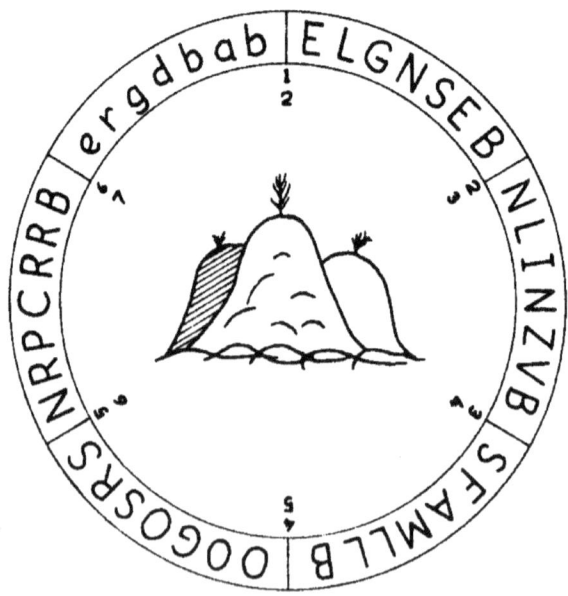

APPENDIX A

17. Dee's meaning is that no description of the spirit was possible, as he had not yet appeared in the stone, unless under another name.

18. The reference here is uncertain. First, we have John Scotus (ERIGENA) c. 850 A.D., of Irish origin. He was employed as teacher at the court of Charles the Bald. His writings included commentaries on Dionysius the Areopagite and a major work entitled *De Divisione Naturae* in which he expounds his leading philosophy, viz. the Unity of Nature, proceeding from God through creative ideas to the sensible universe, ultimately resolved into the First Cause. He was an originator of mystical thought in the Middle Ages.

On the other hand, we have the better known John Duns Scotus (Doctor Subtilis) c. 1265-1308. He was a Scottish theologian and a member of the Franciscan Order of Friars. He was a vigorous supporter of the doctrine of the Immaculate Conception and the freedom of the will. Amongst his works were *De Modis Significandi sive Grammatica Speculativa* (1499), a philosophic grammar, and a work on metaphysics entitled *De Rerum Principio*. He was one of the first to challenge the harmony of faith and reason, a central point in the doctrine of Thomas Aquinas.

In his *Catalogue of Manuscripts*, Dee lists two works under the name Scotus: '*Joh. Duns Scoti quaestiones in Porphyrii quinque voces*' and '*Joh. Scoti quaestiones super secundo et tertio libro Aristotelis de anima*'.

19. Suidas, *Lexicon*, 10th century.

20. St Epiphanius, Bishop of Constantia, d. 403: *De Geranis*.

THE HEPTARCHIA MYSTICA

21. Leviticus VIII, 8 et al.

22. Antonius Mizaldus (Mizauld), *Memorabilium* . (Paris, 1554).

23. In *Quartus Liber Mysteriorum*, the diagram of the 42 Ministers of King Bnapsen contains a devilish face, surrounded by what seem to be flames of fire.

24. *The Table of 49 Good Angels* to be found on the final page of *De Heptarchia Mystica* represents the synthesis of all the forces which comprise this seven-fold system of Magic. The Angelic names which make up the table were first derived in the following manner. On Sunday April 29, 1582, Edward Kelley receives a vision of seven spirits, each holding up a square table divided into 49 lesser squares filled with letters and numbers. The spirits then join their tables together in the form of a cross (see below). In Dee's *Mysteriorum Liber Tertius*, Kelley (then known to Dee as Edward Talbot – see Introduction) relates the vision.

> *All the 7 (which here appear) join their tables in one: which before they held apart. And they be of this form all together. The middlemost is a great square and on each side of it, one as big as it, joining closeth it. And over it joined two, which both together were equal to it: and under it were such other two, as may appear in this little pattern [a small drawing follows]: being thus joined, a bright circle did accompany and enclose them all, thus: but nothing was in the circle.*

APPENDIX A

Kelley then repeats each letter and number to Dee who records them in the following diagram:

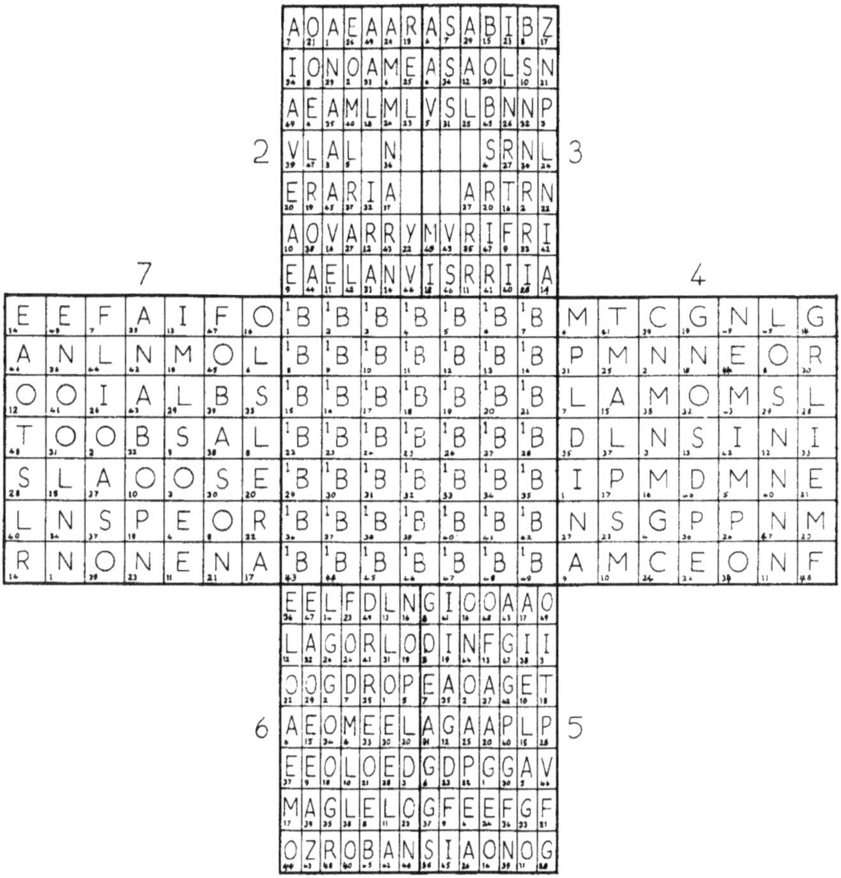

[diagram of cross-shaped grid of letters and numbers]

The names of the 49 good Angels are then extracted from the figure by proceeding in a clockwise manner (beginning in each case with a letter B from the central square numbered 1), and simply observing which letter falls against the relevant

THE HEPTARCHIA MYSTICA

number in each instance. Thus the name of the first Angel follows as

1 in the first square	**B**
1 in the second square	**A**
1 in the third square	**L**
1 in the fourth square	**I**
1 in the fifth square	**G**
1 in the sixth square	**O**
1 in the seventh square	**N**

Therefore the name is **BALIGON**.

Unfortunately, at some point in the past, a small piece of the manuscript has been torn away (or perhaps worm-eaten), obliterating three squares in the second table and five squares in the third. We know this must have occurred before 1672 when the manuscript came into the hands of Elias Ashmole, as his copy bears the same defect. As we possess Dee's collected table of the 49 names, we can easily (by working backwards) rediscover the missing letters and numbers. They are in fact: 15A, 30R and 41A in the second table, and 18I, 19A, 38R, 44G and 48R in the third table. The problem is, however, to what squares do we allocate the rediscovered letters? As the distribution of the letters and numbers throughout the square system is totally random, we are left with six permutations in the case of table 2 and one hundred and twenty permutations in the case of table 3.

Having collected the 49 Angelic names from the seven tables, Dee constructed the following list which he called *Tabula Collecta: 49 Angeloru Bonoru, Nom continens*,[41] from which in turn he formed his circular plan of the system *Tabula Angelorum Bonorum 49*.

APPENDIX A

In Casaubon's edition of the later Diaries I have noticed an instance where *Tabula Collecta* has been employed for the purpose of talismanic magic, details of which are beyond the scope of this present volume.

Tabula Collecta: 49 Angeloru Bonoru, Nom continens [per Δ][42]

1 BALIGON	13 Brisfli	25 Belmara	37 BRALGES
2 BORNORGO	14 Bagnole	26 Benpagi	38 Bormila
3 Bapnido	15 BABALEL	27 Barnafa	39 Buscnab
4 Besgeme	16 BVTMONO	28 Bmilges	40 Bminpol
5 Blumapo	17 Bazpama	29 BNASPOL	41 Bartiro
6 Bmamgal	18 Blintom	30 BRORGES	42 Bliigan
7 Basledf	19 Bragiop	31 Baspalo	43 BLVMAZA
8 BOBOGEL	20 Bermale	32 Binodab	44 BAGENOL
9 BEFAFES	21 Bonefon	33 Bariges	45 Bablibo
10 Basmelo	22 BYNEPOR	34 Binofon	46 Busdana
11 Bernole	23 BLISDON	35 Baldago	47 Blingef
12 Branglo	24 Balceor	36 BNAPSEN	48 Barfort
			49 Bamnode

N.B.: Kings and Princes in capital letters.

---

41. Dee used standard Latin abbreviations in this title. In full it reads:- *Tabula Collecta: 49 Angelorum Bonorum, Nomine continens – A Concise List: Of the 49 Good Angels, Named consecutively.* 'Tabula' is more appropriately rendered as 'list' rather than 'table', as in the manuscript, the angels' names are featured in a single column. [REC]

42. [Per Δ] *(By Dee)*

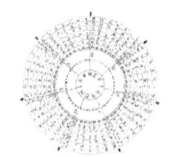

APPENDIX B
JOHN DEE'S RELIGIOUS MAGIC

In order to appreciate John Dee's approach to the magical arts, it is necessary to observe the influences that prevailed during his time and their overall effect on him and his contemporaries.

The philosophical atmosphere of the Elizabethan Renaissance became highly charged with the current of 'new learning' which swept across the known world. An influx of knowledge on a hitherto unprecedented scale brought with it the advancement of ideas, initiating a fervent quest for wisdom and understanding which culminated in the advent of a new being, the Renaissance Magus. With the religious bigotry of the Papal Crown replaced by the scientifically preferable – yet, paradoxically, narrowing – effects of Protestant accession, Tudor England stood on the threshold of a promised Utopia. A new age had dawned.

The emergence of the sixteenth-century Magi gave birth to a great revival of interest in the Hermetic arts of magic, alchemy and the Qabalah: linked with scientific thought, those time-honoured methods were once more to be utilized in a

THE HEPTARCHIA MYSTICA

titanic effort to discover the mysteries of God, Man and Nature.

Though John Dee embraced the whole edifice of the Hermetic corpus, it is evident that his main preoccupation was with magic. Magic, in Dee's view, far divorced from the goetic processes of the medieval grimoires, represented a method by which the Divine Will could be interpreted for the lasting benefit of mankind. The search for the Principle of Unity – lost at the Fall of Man – was of prime importance.

Dee held this factor as the key to all mysteries, ensouling the very nature of the Divinity as comprehended by the spiritually illuminated Adept. To this end it was Dee's ardent wish to communicate with the Angels of Light in an attempt to unravel the complexities of universal law, and restore man to his former estate.

It is immediately obvious to anyone who has studied the Spiritual Diaries in any depth that Dee, although personifying the 'New Age Magus' in every sense, cannot be considered as a magician. Piously Christian, much given to prayer and humility, shunning all that smacked of diabolism or irreverence, John Dee stands curiously alone in the history of occultism. Magical texts of all descriptions existed in Dee's library, but it seems that he never employed them during the Angelic Operations. From various references throughout the *Mysteriorum Libri Quinque* it can be seen that Dee's familiarity with magical books was extensive, often recognizing symbols and references during the actions to have counterparts in the works of Reuchlin and Agrippa, or the book known as *Arbatel*[43]. Despite this, the only

---

43. *The Arbatel of Magic*, trans. Robert Turner 1655, reprinted in the *Fourth Book of Agrippa*, Askins, 1978. *The Arbatel* (first issued at Basel, 1575) contains nine sections or 'tomes', the first of which (*Isagoge*) contains 49 magical aphorisms; other sections deal with Olympic Spirits, Microcosmic Magic, Sibyline Magic etc. Only the first book seems to be extant. [RT]

APPENDIX B

true magical text to be employed extensively throughout the Angelic Operations seems to have been Cornelius Agrippa's *Three Books of Occult Philosophy,* and even so there is little evidence to suggest that this work was used for purposes other than reference. On the other hand, Edward Kelley (as we have seen) was to a certain extent given to the art of conjuration, but here again it is most unlikely that Dee would allow the performance of such rites in his presence.

Having banished the vision of the Solomonic Adept invoking spirits, wand in hand, let us examine what remains. From the outset it seems that prayers to God and the Angels played a major role in the modus of the Dee-Kelley operations. Descriptive passages in the Spiritual Diaries refer to Dee praying in his oratory, while Kelley kneels before the Holy Table and awaits the presence of the Angel. Apart from the occasional recitation of psalms, little else of a ritual nature seems to have transpired. The possible employment of talismans to attract the Angelic forces cannot be overlooked, and, indeed, in the later operations, the presence of the Holy Table, tablets and other items lends credence to this argument. In theory at least, the Holy Table and its furnishings take on a semblance to the Hebrew Ark of the Covenant, with its central 'Mercy Seat', silken trappings and insulation from the earth. Dee is told never to look upon the table without the greatest reverence, and during the Heptarchical workings to approach it with a lamen, or breastplate, over his heart, reminiscent of the High Priest in Exodus. On the appearance of the spirit in the stone, Dee and Kelley are commanded by a mysterious voice (heard only by Kelley) to *'move not, the place is holy'*. This utterance seemed to signal the commencement of the

THE HEPTARCHIA MYSTICA

operation, followed by the appearance of a white cloud within the stone which cleared away at the arrival of the apparitions. The termination of the work seemed entirely dependent on the will of the spirits (unusual in the history of magic), and was indicated by a darkening of the stone. Finally the two offered thanks to the Creator and His servants for their attendance, followed by formal prayers.

It will be seen from the above that the Dee-Kelley approach to Angel-magic bears little resemblance to the techniques laid down by tradition. Gone are the protective and confining circle, the formal invocations, banishings, and licence to depart. Gone are the magical weapons, the tripod of invocations, the triangle of Art, and, to a certain extent, the controlling will of the operator.

The unorthodoxy of Dee's system of Angel-magic is even reflected in the nature and mannerisms of the spirits called into the stone, many of them behaving like a riotous band of elementals, seeming to have more in common with the denizens of *A Midsummer Night's Dream* than those encountered in the field of ritual magic.

(One is reminded of the T.R. and John Cokars' translation of the *Pseudomarchia Daemonum* of Wierus[44] and the delightful invocations of the beautiful fairy Sybilia).

Beyond this, Dee's hierarchy of spiritual beings exhibits an overwhelming obsession with the number seven and its permutations, the letter 'b' (probably the Angelic equivalent of

44. *The Pseudomarchia Daemonum* of Johannes Wierus (Johann Weyer, 1515-1588) is an appendix to his 1577 edition of *De Praestigiis Daemonum* (Basel, 1563). Published during Dee's time, in essence it is a true Elizabethan (and Christianised) grimoire. The text and Sybilia's invocations were later included in Reginald Scot's *Discovery of Witchcraft* (1584). The identity of its translator 'T.R.' is unknown, yet it is certain that John Cokars was somehow involved. Several variant spellings of the name Cokars appear in Dee's Diaries and other works, i.e. Croker, Crockers, Crockars. [RT]

APPENDIX B

the number seven), and possessing virtually unpronounceable names. Dee's spirits also proved to be remarkably accomplished musicians, exhibiting amazing dexterity as they played tuneful melodies upon pyramidal shaped trumpets and bulbous forty-nine holed flutes (*Quartus Liber Mysteriorum*)! It is also clear that the virtues of brevity and straightforwardness were not inherent in the natures of these strange creatures. Poor Dee must have been driven half mad by the longwinded and laboriously complicated methods which the spirits employed to transmit simple facts.

With particular reference to *De Heptarchia Mystica* several other striking peculiarities emerge. Firstly, we have the matter of unstable personalities: Carmara (or Marmara) becomes Baligon; while Hagonel, with the substitution of B for H and transposition of O and E, would seem to become Bagenol. This explains to some extent Dee's note regarding Bagenol in Chapter 4 of the *Heptarchia*. 'He appeared not *by that name yet*'. This transference of identity extends in a certain manner to other spirits in the system in a way so far unexplained, but further research may yield an answer.

Consideration of the planetary attributions allocated to the Heptarchical Kings and Princes gives rise to further confusion. While the Kings follow the traditional order of planetary ascriptions assigned to the days of the week, the Princes do not. A conflicting series of associations emerges which – to my knowledge – has no traditional counterpart. This is further complicated by the inclusion of Carmara (Baligon)/Venus, and Hagonel (Bagenol)/Moon under the headings of both Monday and Friday (see Chapter 7 of Dee's text). The astrological attributions given in Dee's manuscript are as follows:

THE HEPTARCHIA MYSTICA

Day	KING	Planet	PRINCE	Planet
Sunday	Bobogel	Sun	Bornogo	Venus
Monday	Blvmaza[45]	Moon	Bralges[46]	Saturn
Tuesday	Babalel	Mars	Befafes	Sun
Wednesday	Bnaspol	Mercury	Blisdon	Jupiter
Thursday	Bynepor	Jupiter	Bvtmono	Mars
Friday	Baligon	Venus	Bagenol	Moon
Saturday	Bnapsen	Saturn	Brorges	Mercury

Strange bedfellows indeed. One would expect the qualities of each King to be reflected in his respective Prince, so why this conflict of planetary designation? The astrological incompatibility of the Kings and Princes does not; however, seem to extend to their powers and dominions, each pair exhibiting similar characteristics. Once again a chaotic picture emerges, however, with **BABALEL** and **BEFAFES** ruling the Sea (Fire and Fire astrologically, Fire and Water fatalistically), Bnaspol and Blisdon ruling Earth (Air and Water astrologically, Water and Water fatalistically) and so forth. While it is uncertain what to make of these seemingly contradictory elements in Dee's system, perhaps it is easier to consider the Prince in each case as a component part of his King as reflected in Dee's note in *Quartus Liber Mysteriorum*. 'My Prince is in myself, which is a mystery'.

Although no definite system of planetary hours is ascribed to the Heptarchical Angels, we read in Chapter 3 of Dee's text: '*The King and the Prince govern for the whole day. The rest according to the six parts of the day*'. 'The rest' are apparently the 42 Ministers of each Prince. By way of explanation Dee gives the following diagram in the *Liber Mysteriorum Quartus*.

45. Carmara is also given for this day. [RT]   46. Hagonel is also given for this day. [RT]

APPENDIX B

E [47]		
OFSNGLE	4 hours	
AVZNILN	4 hours	
YLLMAFS	4 hours	
		= 24 hours
NRSOGOO	4 hours	
NRRCPRN	4 hours	
LABDGRE	4 hours	

The example is of the 42 Ministers of Prince Hagonel (Bagenol), each letter representing a spirit (see Appendix A, Note 4) each line of seven spirits therefore rules four hours of the day. The names are generated, as we have mentioned elsewhere, from a method which combines (therefore represents) the letters of the forty-nine Angels, both called and uncalled.

The Heptarchical operation itself seems to be a simple technique when compared with other magical systems. After deciding the forces to be invoked, and with due observation of the correct day for their summoning, the operator sets up the Holy Table in the prescribed manner (see Appendix A, Note 7). On the ground before the table he places the appropriate circular table of the 42 Ministers (Appendix A, Note 4), and covers the same with a tablet containing the seal of their Prince, upon which he stands. He must have the Lamen upon his breast and the ring upon his finger. Holding in his hands a circular wooden tablet bearing the sigil of the relevant Heptarchical King, he reads aloud the oration which begins 'O Almighty, Æternal, the true and living God . . .' (see Chapter 5), followed by the Exordium of the King, and finally that of the Prince

47. This E is Dee's correction and replaces F in the manuscript. [RT]

THE HEPTARCHIA MYSTICA

(see Chapter 6). At the conclusion of the operation thanks are offered to God, and the Angels who have attended.

As we do not know the offices or the powers of the seven spiritual Ministers that preside in each four-hour cycle, it is impossible to be precise regarding the time of the operation. It seems that the spirits communicate by a form of telepathy accompanied by visions in the crystal or shew-stone. It is unknown whether incense, holy water, or ceremonial robes were to be employed.

It has been argued in recent years that Dee's entire system of Angelic magic is in reality a cipher, or even a complex method of encipherment employed during his activities with the Elizabethan 'secret service'; the magical element being included as a red herring to throw his opponents off the track. Much of this reasoning stems from the fact that Dee bought a copy of the much sought-after *Steganographia* of Abbot Trithemius[48] while travelling in the Low Countries during 1562. The *Steganographia*, as D. P. Walker has pointed out[49], is in fact a book concerning various methods of encipherment disguised as a treatise on Angel magic. Although this work most probably gave Dee much food for thought, the nature and content of the Spiritual Diaries makes it most unlikely that a similar method was involved as Donald Laycock admirably demonstrates in his *Complete Enochian Dictionary*.[50] Another work of Trithemius' known as *Polygraphia* (published 1516), which may have influenced Dee, contains hundreds of substitution ciphers in the form of poly-alphabets which yield structures similar to

---

48. *The Steganographia of Johannes Trithemius*, tr. Fiona Tait and Christopher Upton; edited with an introduction by Adam McLean, Edinburgh: Magnum Opus Hermetic Sourceworks, 1982. 49. D. P. Walker. *Spiritual and Demonic Magic* (from *Ficino to Campanella*), London, 1969. 50. Donald C. Laycock. *The Complete Enochian Dictionary*, York Beach, ME: Weiser, 2001.

APPENDIX B

those encountered in *De Heptarchia Mystica*. For example, the words JOHN DEE enciphered with Trithemius' *Tabula Recta* (square table) system yield JPKQ DFG. No-one can be quite certain about these matters but in my view – based upon fourteen years of research – Dee's magical writings are what they appear to be and do not involve a system of cryptography. Even *De Heptarchia Mystica*, the prime candidate upon which to base the 'cipher theory' firmly resists any attempts at cryptoanalysis.

Although throughout his long life John Dee insisted that he neither saw nor heard the apparitions that so haunted him, he nevertheless wrote in his private diary on May 25, 1581: 'I had sight in crystallo offered me, and I saw'. The word 'crystallo' he had transliterated into Greek in an attempt to conceal its meaning. Had Dee something to hide? Did he really see spirits, but was afraid to admit the fact, even to himself? On this matter, perhaps we should leave the final word to Puck: after all, he should know!

'If we shadows have offended,
Think but this (and all is mended),
That you have but slumber'd here,
While these visions did appear.'

(Puck's speech, *A Midsummer Night's Dream*, Act V, Scene 1, Line 2275)

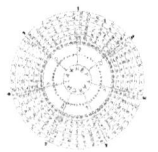

APPENDIX C
MORTLAKE REVISTED[51]
BY ROBIN E. COUSINS

In Mortlake today, there is little trace of its famous resident, John Dee. His house no longer exists and his gravestone in the chancel of the parish church of St Mary the Virgin has long gone. The only immediately obvious reminder is John Dee House, the name of a modern block of flats standing on the site of Dee's garden, immediately west of the church in Mortlake High Street.

Dee 'dwelt in a house neere the water side a little westward from the church'[52] on the opposite side of the High Street. The road, in fact, separated most of the garden from the house. The garden was accessed by a 'great gate' from the High Street and was part of the common fields of Mortlake that extended southwards from the High Street for one and a half miles into Richmond Park. Dee's house stood approximately to the west of the present Tapestry Court, a grassed area between the High

---

51. This is the third revised edition. The article first appeared in the 2nd edition of the *Heptarchia Mystica* (1986) and was later rewritten and abridged for the *Talking Stick Magickal Journal*, Issue 1, Vol. II, (1998), pp. 54-6.   52. *Elias Ashmole, His Autobiographical and Historical Notes, His Correspondence and Other Contemporary Sources relating to his Life and Work*, 1966, Vol. IV, p. 1333.

THE HEPTARCHIA MYSTICA

Street and the Thames Towing Path with seating overlooking the river. Originally known as Queens Head Court and later Tapestry Alley, this area was once a narrow passage with a middle courtyard. Part of the famous Mortlake Tapestry Works, known locally as Lower Dutch House, was located on the east side of the alleyway and the former Queens Head Inn stands to the north-west on the river-bank. The stairs leading down to the foreshore from the towing path at the bottom of Tapestry Court are possibly the 'Watergate Stayres' that Arthur Dee fell down at 12.15 p.m. on July 3, 1582, cutting 'his forhed on the right eyebrow' – an incident John Dee recorded in his diary.[53]

John Dee was settled in Mortlake by 1570. He was travelling in Europe with Edward Kelley between 1583 and 1589. Later, on February 20, 1596, he was installed as Warden of Christ's College, Manchester, a post he held until November 1604. Thereafter, he returned to Mortlake, where he remained until his death in 1609.[54]

Dee's house was possibly built during the reign of Henry VII (1485-1509) and originally belonged to his mother, Johanna Wild. On 15 June 1579, she signed over the house and lands to him and his descendants. A charge of twenty shillings was required for the transfer, which was paid on 30 October 1579. Johanna Dee lived with Dee and his family for the rest of her life, dying in October 1580 aged seventy-seven. Dee gradually extended the premises by the purchase of adjoining small tenements that were subsequently developed to house his laboratory and library.

---

53. John Dee, *The Private Diary*, edited by James Orchard Halliwell,(1842), p. 16. Arthur Dee (1579-1651) was John Dee's eldest son. 54. Some sources suggest Dee may have died at the house of his friend John Pontois in Bishopgate Street in the City of London. Nevertheless, his body still had to be transported back to Mortlake for burial.

APPENDIX C

A contemporary description of the property is provided by a survey of Mortlake, dated 1617, then part of the Manor of Wimbledon. The surveyor was Ralph Treswell (c.1540-1616/17), who was assisted by a specially appointed jury of thirteen. The survey moved westward along the north side of Mortlake High Street, eventually arriving at a 'howse with yarde and garden Plot' and an 'auncient messuage with owthouses, orchard and garden', separated by a square court.[55]

The 'howse with yarde' was the laboratory, while the 'messuage' to the west of the court was the Dee family home, which at the time of the survey belonged to the descendants of one Bartholomew Brickwood, who had bought the property on Dee's death in 1609. The old laboratory building stood on land belonging to a Mr John Juxon that was acquired by Sir Francis Crane (c.1579 - c.1636) in 1619 for the purpose of founding the Mortlake Tapestry Works. Crane, a distinguished courter, had received a subsidy of £2,000 from James I in order to establish the manufactory, which was built forthwith 'upon the Ground whereon Doctor Dees laboratory (& other Roomes for that use) stood'.[56]

Elias Ashmole (1617-1692), who was 'in quest of whatsoever Doctor Dee left behind him', asked the antiquary John Aubrey (1627-1697) to seek out a local contemporary of Dee for an account of the Doctor. In early January 1673, Aubrey was directed to the Goodwife Faldo, an eighty-two year old native of Mortlake. Ashmole received Aubrey's report on the 27 January, but finding it unsatisfactory, interviewed the Goodwife Faldo

---

55. Maurice Stanley Cockin, *A Story-Book about Mortlake and her Church*, 1954, p. 98.   56. Ashmole, op. cit., p. 1333   57. From Hippocrates Junior [Major J.Waller], *The Predicted Plague*, London, 1900. Never verified as an accurate depiction of Dee's house, the sketch was from the collection of antiquary William Upcott (1779-1845) which was sold by Sotheby after his death.

THE HEPTARCHIA MYSTICA

'A rough sketch of Dee's House at Mortlake', possibly early 19th century.[57]

himself on 11 August 1673. The two accounts cover much the same ground, although Ashmole's report is more ordered.[58]

The Goodwife Faldo knew Dee well and often visited his house, which to confirm its location, was next to a square court west of the 'howse where wthe Tapistry hangings are made'. In 1673 the house was occupied by a Mr Selbury. Dee had four or five rooms in his house 'filled with bookes' and he kept 'a great many Stille' in which he used 'an abundance of Eggeshells'. He kept a 'plentifull Table and a good Howse' and once showed Faldo and her mother (who 'dwelt neere him, in the same Towne') the Ecclips of the Sun in one of his Roomes, which he had made darke'

---

58. Ashmole, op. cit., pp. 1298-1300, 1332-35. The quotations in the following paragraph are taken from both reports.

APPENDIX C

Nevertheless, despite the reports of Treswell and the Goodwife Faldo, the precise location of Dee's house is still by no means certain. In 2000, archaeological excavations were undertaken between 13 November and 22 December and between 10 September and 10 October 2001 in the area around the possible site of Dee's house and the tapestry works. New luxury riverside flats with a basement car park were going to be built in the vicinity and the excavations were required to preserve and record the archaeology of the historic area. The work was supervised by Lorraine Darton and the pre-construct archaeology reports were summarised in her article, 'Insights into the development of medieval and post-medieval riverside buildings at Mortlake.'[59] The excavations were described as having been

> 'recently undertaken on two riverside sites along the north side of Mortlake High Street, in an area where the 16th century mathematician Dr John Dee once resided, and where Flemish weavers produced works for Charles I in the 17th century at the Mortlake tapestry works. A succession of late medieval and post-medieval buildings was discovered on plots between the River Thames and Mortlake High Street, in the London Borough of Richmond-upon-Thames. Two pits, a ditch and a structure, represented by stakeholes and postholes, pre-dated the late medieval buildings. The excavations revealed a complex sequence of floor surfaces and wall footings of houses, outbuildings and drains that once stood here' (p.231).

Disappointingly, the excavation was unable to identify with any certainty, structural remains that could be described as being Dee's house. The conclusion was:

59. Published in *Surrey Archaeological Collections*. Vol. 91 (2004), pp. 231-61.

THE HEPTARCHIA MYSTICA

'While no direct evidence of the house of Dr John Dee exists, the indications of domestic activity and a structure possibly dating to the Tudor period, along with documentary evidence [i.e., the reports from Treswell and Ashmole] placing the dwelling in the vicinity, suggests these discoveries could be linked to one of his buildings' (p. 240).

When Dee was in Europe, his house was ransacked by the Clerks of the Records in the Tower. He had mistakenly entrusted 'all my household stuff' to his brother-in-law, Nicholas Fromond, who 'unduly sold it presently, or caused it to be carried away upon my departure'. Meanwhile the Clerks of the Records in the Tower 'satt whole dayes at my house in Mortlake, in gathering rarities to their liking', which were removed allegedly for the payments of debts that Dee had accrued. Upon his return in December 1589, a shocked Dee reported his losses to a specially appointed commission in 1592. Totalling £1510, the costs claimed included £100 for 'my furniture of Laboratories'; £30 for 'Mathematical Instruments' including a lost Quadrant and 'Astronomer's staff'; £10 for a 'Magnes-stone'; and £150 for over 500 missing books and manuscripts.[60]

After the Tapestry Manufactory closed in 1703, the original Queens Head Inn was built between Dee's old house and the Thames on land belonging to the factory. One can imagine that Dee would hardly have been amused to find the inn on his orchard and the view of the river obscured. The inn was eventually demolished and rebuilt in 1885. It was closed down permanently in 1952 and converted into flats.

---

60. For full details of Dee's losses, the damage to his property, and his attempts to gain compensation, see, 'The Compendious Rehearsal of John Dee' (1593. in Thomas Hearne, *Johannis Glastoniensis Chronica*, Oxford, 1726, pp. 529-35.

APPENDIX C

In 1814 the house was a Ladies' Boarding School administered by a Mrs Dubois and it had contained, a few years previously, a room 'ornamented with red and white roses [61]'. Sir Richard Phillips (1767-1840) visited the school in 1816, being unable to resist his 'curiosity to view the house in which he [Dee] resided'. Mrs Dubois starchily showed him through the principal rooms.

> *'In two hundred years, it has, of course, undergone considerable alterations: yet parts of it exhibit the architecture of the sixteenth century. From the front windows I was shown Dee's garden, on the other side of the road, still attached [i.e. belonging] to the house; down the central path of which, through iron gates, yet standing, Queen Elizabeth used to walk from her carriage...'* [62]

On September 17, 1580, Dee records one such visitation in his diary:

> *'The Quene's Majestie cam from Rychemond in her coach, the higher way of Mortlak felde, and whan she cam right against the church she turned down toward my howse: and when she was against my garden in the felde she stode there a good while, and then cam ynto the street at the great gate of the felde, where she espyed me at my doore .'* [63]

The 'great gate of the felde' with globe topped posts can be seen in the eighteenth century print of Mortlake Church on the right beneath the Queen's Head Inn sign that is suspended across the High Street to the house where the artist of the Tapestry Works once lived.

61. Owen Manning, *Antiquities of the County of Surrey*, 1814. Vol. 3, p 304. 62. Sir Richard Phillips, *A Morning's Walk from London to Kew*, 2nd edition, 1820, p. 275. 63. Dee, *The Private Diary*, p. 8.

THE HEPTARCHIA MYSTICA

'*The North View of Mortlake Church*' (1750) by Jean-Baptiste-Claude Chatelain (1710-58).

The 'great gate of the felde' and paling fence.

Some of the garden was fenced with pales, when Dee possessed it, and a brick wall separated his garden from the church.[64] It is possible that part of the garden wall of his property is incorporated into the western wall of St Mary's churchyard

64. Charles Hailstone, *Alleyways of Mortlake and East Sheen*, 1983, p. 55.

APPENDIX C

that separates the church from the modern John Dee House. A plaque has been attached to the wall to that effect – 'The central part of this wall, visible from the churchyard path, may be the last physical remnant of John Dee's property'.

The house for the limner or artist of the Tapestry Works, previously referred to, was built on part of the garden next to the churchyard wall (see print) and a row of houses, known as Victoria Terrace, was erected on the remainder during the nineteenth century. When John Dee House was built in 1957,

The possible remains of John Dee's Garden Wall.
(Photograph© R.E. Cousins)

THE HEPTARCHIA MYSTICA

the site was cleared, even removing an old iron gateway in the garden wall at the rear, possibly the same gateway which Phillips saw in 1816.

John Dee House (Photograph © R.E. Cousins)

Building development along the High Street during the nineteenth century would have enclosed Dee's house. During the 1849 cholera epidemic, Mortlake was severely afflicted, especially in the vicinity of Queens Head Court, where the medical officer reported a privy in a most revolting state.[65]

The Dee house, however, was soon a memory. For in 1886, John Anderson (1844-1915), a local historian, wrote that there

65. Charles Marshall Rose, Nineteenth Century Mortlake and East Sheen, 1961, p. 38.

APPENDIX C

was 'a stone let into the wall up the Court marking the site of his house'.[66] However, massive redevelopment during the twentieth century ensured the disappearance of this commemorative stone in Tapestry Court, but luckily a new plaque is now affixed to the wall of the former Queen's Head Inn, stating: 'This building, formerly the Queen's Head Inn, was built on the site of part of John Dee's house, library and laboratory'. The widening of Mortlake High Street in post-war years resulted in many buildings being demolished. The Tapestry House or Lower Dutch House, which stood on the site of Dee's laboratory, became a tenement house after the closure of the factory, but in 1951 it was declared dangerous and demolished. A plaque set in the ground at Tapestry Court marks the site, but fails to mention Dee.

Tapestry Court and the former Queen's Head (Photograph© R.E. Cousins)

66. John Eustace Anderson, *A History, of the Parish of Mortlake*, 1886, p. 26.

THE HEPTARCHIA MYSTICA

Plaque in Tapestry Court (Photograph© R.E. Cousins)

When John Dee died in 1609, he was buried in the chancel of Mortlake Parish Church. However, seekers of his memorial are doomed to disappointment. Sir Richard Phillips failed in 1816, as did John Anderson, who scoured in vain the Vestry Minutes Books of the first decade of the seventeenth century for a record of the fee of 6s.8d, for Dee's interment in the church. [67]

Unfortunately, a Register of Burials was not maintained between 1603 and 1613. Yet again, the Goodwife Faldo solves the mystery, informing Ashmole and Aubrey that Dee 'lyes buried in the Chancell of Mortlack Church about the midle yet neerer the South side, between the Graves of Mr Holt & Mr Myles, who haue grauestones with Inscriptions upon them. There also lay an old Grauestone upon him'. [68]

---

67. Anderson, p. 29.
68. Ashmole, op. cit., p. 1333 and pp. 1298-1300, 1334-5 for all quotations following.

APPENDIX C

The old marble stone bore no inscription, but '2 or 3 brasse pinnes' remained from the brass which had been removed 'long before 'Doctor Dee's buriall'. When the floor of the chancel was layd flatt in Olivers [Cromwell's] time', Dee's second-hand gravestone was removed to the entrance of the chancel, where it must have remained until the chancel was rebuilt in 1885. The brass inscriptions from the graves of Anthony Holt (d. 1602) and Edward Myles (d. 1618), who were both 'servants to Queen Elizabeth', were transferred to the walls of the church, but Dee's old stone must have disappeared in the rubble.

In 1906 the galleries in the church were removed. The West Gallery had been provided by John Dee. The carpenter was the father of the Goodwife Faldo and in the south end of the gallery was carved Dee's identifying Delta and the installation date thus:

$$1590$$
$$\Delta$$

However, all is not lost. Dee's red and gold coat of arms with a rampant lion can be seen in the chancel on the panelling to the right of the altar. Moreover, in 2013, the John Dee of Mortlake Society (2009-18) commissioned a memorial plaque for Dee. Carved in Welsh slate by Julia Hoffnung, it is on the south wall near to where the Goodwife Faldo maintained Dee was interred.

John Dee's Coat of Arms, Mortlake Church

To help conjure up the presence of John Dee in Mortlake today,

THE HEPTARCHIA MYSTICA

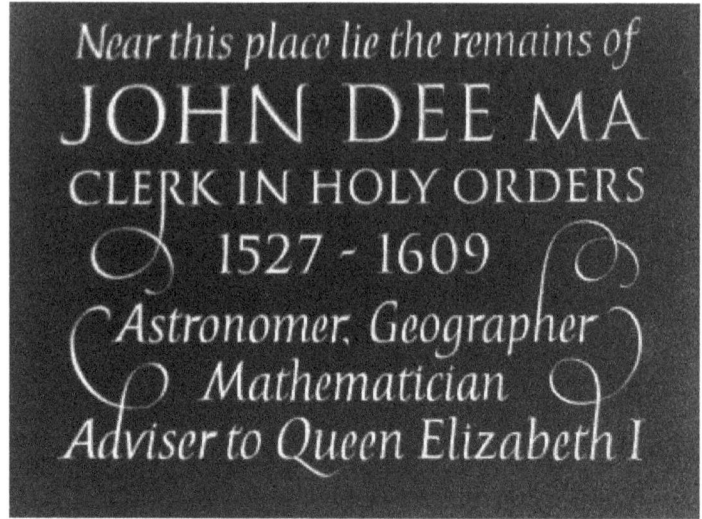

John Dee's Memorial Plaque, Mortlake Church

some last reminiscences from the Goodwife Faldo, as retold by Ashmole and Aubrey, may help. Dee walked '*very upright, without a staff, with his hands behind him, while about home. He was tall, and wore his beard picked [i.e. long and pointed], being very white*'. He dressed in a '*black gowne still with long sleeves, with slitts but without Buttons and loops and tufts*'. Children dreaded Dee '*because he was counted a conjuror*' and, after his death, they would '*runne to Doctor Dees stone*' when they played in the church. Nevertheless, Dee was considered a great peacemaker by his neighbours and long after his death they desired a '*Peacemaker such as Doctor Dee was*' during disputes.

The Goodwife Faldo died in 1674, her burial being recorded in the Mortlake Parish Register on 30 March.

APPENDIX C

BIBLIOGRAPHY FOR APPENDIX C

ANDERSON, John Eustace.
History of the Parish of Mortlake. London, 1983. Facsimile of the 1886 edition.
Mortlake Parish Vestry Minute Book 1578-1652. Privately printed, 1914.
Mortlake, Surrey: Rambles of Old Waxam, the Cobbler. Privately printed, 1909.
Short account of the Tapestry Works, Mortlake. Privately printed, 1894.

ASHMOLE, Elias. *His autobiographical and historical notes, his correspondence and other contemporary sources relating to his life and work; ed.* by C. H. Josten. 5 vols. Oxford, 1966.

BARNES & MORTLAKE HISTORY SOCIETY.
Barnes and Mortlake as it was. Hendon Mill, Lancs, 1977.
Glimpses of Old Barnes and Mortlake. Hendon Mill, 1984.
Vanished houses of Barnes, Mortlake and East Sheen. 1978.
Vintage Barnes and Mortlake. Hendon Mill, 1979.

CHATELAIN, Jean-Baptiste-Claude. *Fifty small and original and elegant views of the most splendid churches, villages, rural prospects adjacent to London.* London, 1750.

COCKIN, Maurice Stanley. *A story-book about Mortlake and her church.* Privately printed, 1954.
COCKIN, Maurice Stanley and Gould, David (eds.). *Mortlake Parish Register 1599-1678.* Borough of Barnes History Society, 1958.

DARTON, Lorraine. 'Insights into the development of medieval and post-medieval riverside buildings at Mortlake.' *Surrey Archaeological Collections*, 91 (2004), pp. 231-61.

DEE, John. *The Private Diary*, ed. by James Orchard Halliwell. London: Camden Society, 1842.

FRENCH, Peter J. *John Dee: The World of an Elizabethan Magus.* London, 1972.

HAILSTONE, Charles. *Alleyways of Mortlake and East Sheen.* Barnes & Mortlake History Society, 1983.

MANNING, Owen. *Antiquities of the County of Surrey.* London, 1814.

PHILLIPS, Sir Richard. *A morning's walk from London to Kew.* 2nd ed., London, 1820.

ROSE, Charles Marshall. *Nineteenth Century Mortlake and East Sheen.* Privately printed, 1961.

SMITH, Charlotte Fell. *John Dee: 1527-1608.* London, 1909.

YEANDLE, W. H. *History of the Churches in Mortlake and East Sheen.* Richmond & Barnes, 1925.

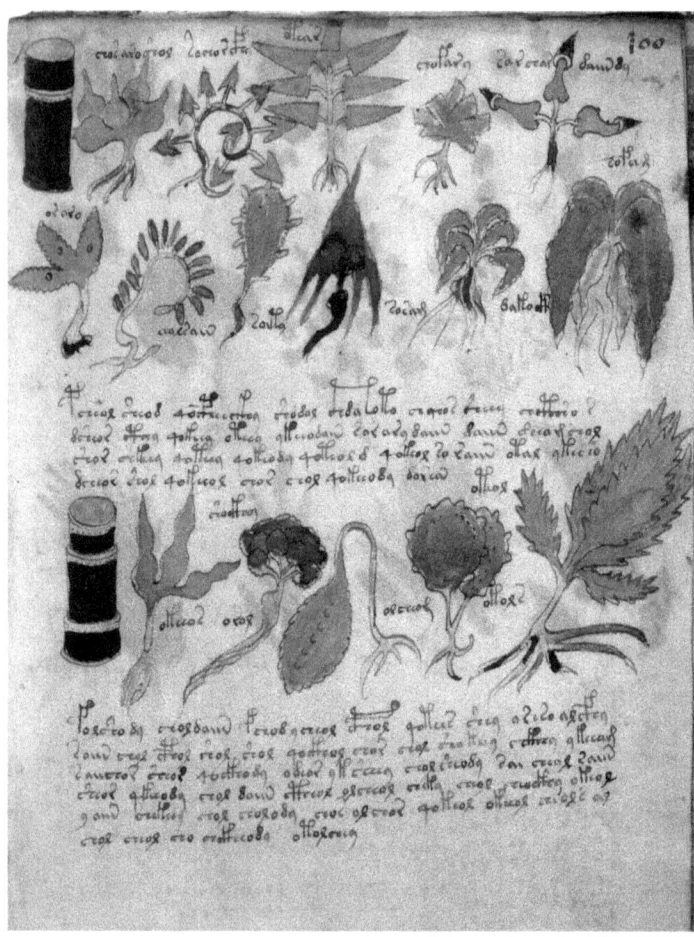

Folio 100r fom the Voynich Manuscript. Reproduced by permission of the Beinecke Rare Book and Manuscript Library, Yale University, Connecticut.

APPENDIX D
THE VOYNICH MANUSCRIPT AND AN ANCIENT TREASURE MAP

In 1912 Wilfred Voynich (1865-1930), a former Polish revolutionary and an antiquarian book dealer in London and New York, acquired a unique and most mysterious manuscript from the Collegium Romanum, an Italian Jesuit School near Rome. Although the document proved to be unreadable, being written in a seemingly unbreakable code, Voynich purchased the codex as part of a group of 30 manuscripts and thus presented to the world what has proved to be the 'Mount Everest' for cryptanalysts.[69]

At first glance Voynich's manuscript appears to be written in a normal flowing longhand penned by an unhesitating scribe; closer scrutiny, however, reveals a text in no known language, which obstinately refuses to give up its secrets despite the laborious efforts of the world's finest code-breakers.

The leaves of the manuscript are of high quality vellum

---

69. The Collegium was located in the Villa Mondragone (built in 1573), about 20 km south-east of Rome. In need of funds, the school was quietly selling some of its holdings and Voynich was sworn to secrecy about the sale. The truth emerged after his death. The Collegium closed in 1953. [REC]

THE HEPTARCHIA MYSTICA

measuring six inches by nine inches and contain a text written in black ink, together with a large number of illustrations in red, blue, green, yellow and brown. The opening section of the manuscript is illustrated with drawings largely botanical in nature – one plant to each page – followed by a host of representations of nude females (who appear to be bathing), finally giving way to a series of star-maps and asterisms. Two hundred and four pages remain extant, though experts estimate some thirty pages to be missing owing to indications found in the binding. Untitled, coverless, and unread, the manuscript now resides in the collection of the Beinecke Rare Book and Manuscript Library, Yale University, Connecticut, awaiting a translator capable of unravelling its mysteries.

As we shall see later, some progress has recently been made in deciphering the code employed in the Voynich text, but before we enlarge upon this matter I think it would be well to furnish the reader with a brief account of the history of the Voynich manuscript and its possible connection with John Dee.

Although some authorities date the manuscript at approximately 1500, others with equally sound reasoning attribute the work to the English Franciscan Friar Roger Bacon, who lived in the thirteenth century (1214-1294?). Bacon, an alchemist, inventor and early scientist, has been accredited with the invention of the microscope, the telescope, gunpowder, and – amongst other things – the creation of a talking automaton in the form of a robotic brazen head. Bacon is also known to be the author of several alchemical and chemical tracts written in cipher. John Dee possessed most of Bacon's better known works, and followed the early Baconian tradition with

APPENDIX D

regard to the qualities of the vegetable and mineral kingdoms, and – as we have seen – also shared a common interest in the mechanical arts. A belief in the possibility of conveying a semblance of life and intelligence to machines through magical means was almost universally held in medieval and Elizabethan times.

The attribution of the Voynich manuscript to Roger Bacon was first recorded by Jan Marek Marci (1595-1667),[70] the rector of the University of Prague, who related that the document had been purchased by Emperor Rudolf II during the late sixteenth century. During this period John Dee and Edward Kelley were frequent visitors to the Prague court of the Emperor, and it is quite possible that Dee, knowing of Rudolf's interest in Friar Bacon's alchemical writings, had sold the manuscript to his host. It is alleged that Rudolf paid the vast sum of 600 golden ducats for the text.

It has been said that John Dee could have obtained the manuscript from the Duke of Northumberland (Dee was tutor to the children of the Duke and in his *Mathematicall Preface to Euclid* he extols the virtues of the Duke's eldest son, the Earl of Warwick), who sacked many monasteries at the order of King Henry VIII.

In the first spiritual diary (1582), Dee refers to one of his books by the name of *Soyga,* which he is unable to read. However, it was not the Voynich manuscript. Elias Ashmole considered the book *Soyga* and Dee's complex volume of tables *Liber Loagaeth,* or the *Book of Enoch,* to be one and the same text, but seems to have ignored the fact that *Soyga* was referred to as an extant text two years before the advent of *Liber Loagaeth.* Dee's son Arthur also refers to a book 'containing nought

70. Aka Johannes Marcus Marci [REC].

THE HEPTARCHIA MYSTICA

but hieroglyphicks', to which his father devoted much study during his time in Prague, but which he could not decipher.

In the later books of the *Mysteriorum Libri Quinque*, Dee indicates that the *Book of Soyga* — now rediscovered — is a work that could only be assailed by inspiration, something which lay just below the level of the conscious mind, the tip-of-the-tongue situation which to this day epitomizes the Voynich enigma.[71]

Work on the Voynich codex conducted by Robert S. Brumbaugh in 1975/76 provides a partial solution to the mystery that surrounds the manuscript, or at least to the code employed. By utilizing a 9 x 4 box substitution method as a grid system, Mr Brumbaugh seems to have successfully solved the involved cipher, but adds: `... the reader need have no fear that the solution will remove all mystery and ambiguity from the manuscript: it turns out to be one thing to solve the cipher and quite another to edit, translate, and interpret the resulting plain text.'[72]

In short, although Brumbaugh's 'solution' provides useful clues to the evaluation of individual words in the codex, we are in reality no nearer to reading the plain text, which proves to be a polylingual jumble never before encountered. What does emerge from Robert Brumbaugh's work is that the manuscript is most likely alchemical, or, as he puts it, '... a treatise on the Elixir of Life'. This conclusion is of course precisely what would be expected if the work indeed originated from Roger

71. Long thought lost, two copies of the 16th century *Book of Soyga* were located by Dee scholar Deborah Harkness in the British Library (BL Sloane MS 8) and the Bodleian Library (Bodley MS 908) under the title *Aldaraia sive Soyga vocor*. A translation from the Latin by Jane Kupin (2014), who utilised both manuscripts, is available to download as a pdf from www.esotericarchives.com .[REC]. 72. Robert S. Brumbaugh. *The Solution of the Voynich 'Roger Bacon' Cipher*. Yale University Library Gazette, 1975, p. 347.

APPENDIX D

Bacon. In the course of his studies, Brumbaugh has brought to light material which would seem to conflict with the Roger Bacon attribution, in as much as certain New World plants have been identified in the codex (the sunflower and the capsicum pepper, first brought to Europe by Columbus in 1493). However, as Brumbaugh himself points out, '... this says nothing about the date of the material in this treatise, nor the attribution to Roger Bacon.'[73] Could these items, therefore, have been added to the text at some later date?

During 1666 Athanasius Kircher, the learned Jesuit scholar, received the manuscript from his pupil Marci who hoped his master would afford a solution to the cryptogram. As with his efforts regarding the ancient Egyptian hieroglyphics, Kircher failed utterly.

Without further appraisal and verification, it is difficult to say whether or not Brumbaugh's conclusions bring us nearer to the truth than Kircher's. In addition, the involvement of both Roger Bacon and John Dee with what has been termed 'the world's most mysterious manuscript' remains unproven to this day. The facts which have so far emerged do seem powerfully to imply such an involvement and, if this proves to be the case, the final solution may well rest with the occultist rather than the cryptanalyst.

---

73. Robert S. Brumbaugh, "The Voynich 'Roger Bacon' Cipher Manuscript: Deciphered Maps of the Stars", *Journal of the Warburg and Courtauld Institutes*, Vol. 39 (1976), p. 139.

THE HEPTARCHIA MYSTICA

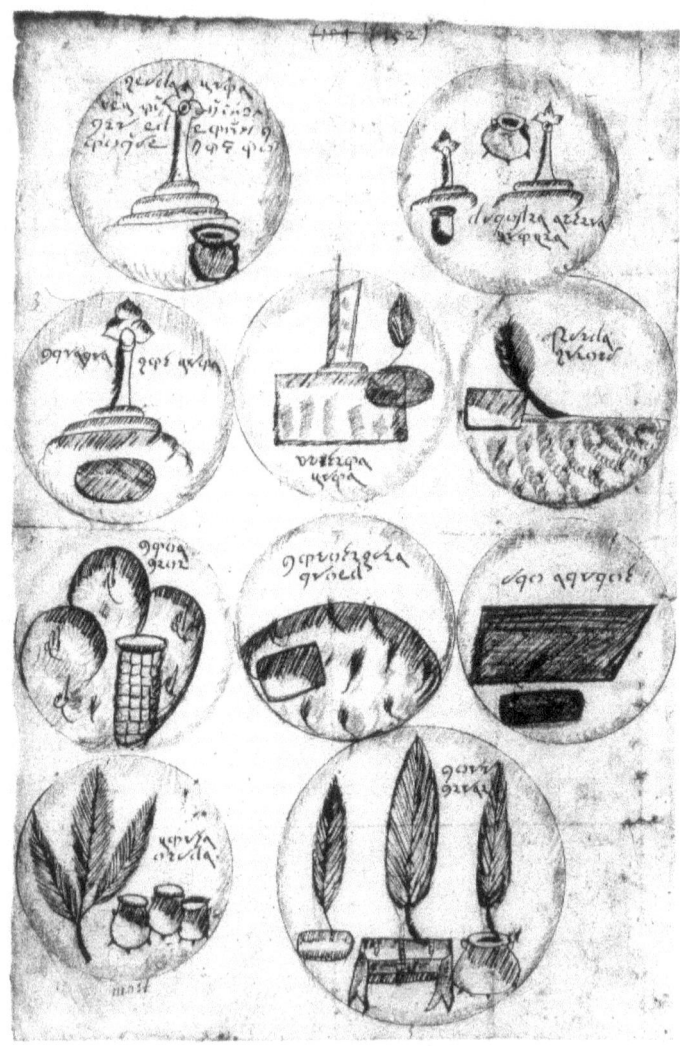

Edward Kelley's Treasure Map.
© British Library Board (BL Sloane 3188, fol. 86v).

APPENDIX D

John Dee's deep interest in cipher systems is further emphasized by an event which took place in April 1582 when Edward Kelley returned from a visit to Blockley in the Cotswolds with a scroll containing a mysterious map delineated in ten circles – drawn in 'silver point', the Elizabethan equivalent of black lead – containing words written in a strange cipher along with crude drawings[74] of crosses and other items, including the following text in the same cipher.

The Cipher Text

After some deliberation Dee guessed the cryptogram to be in Latin and devised a substitutional alphabet.

a b c d e f g h i k l m n o p q r s t v w x y z

Dee's solution to the cipher, as he transcribed it

---

74. These included a 'certayne moniment of a boke' on magic and alchemy (*The Book of St Dunstan*) and the red powder of projection in a hollow stone that Kelley did not admit to finding until 18th April, and which would later guarantee continuing patronage during the travels across Europe in the 1580s. [REC]

THE HEPTARCHIA MYSTICA

The following text was the result:
Tabula locorum rerum et thesaurorum absconditorum Menaboni mei, Gordanigi[75] militis et Danaorum principis expulsi, multorumque aliorum clarissimorum (Britanie meridionali parte) virorum, contra eiusdem inhabitationes militantium: quam hic, familiarissimorum consensu, aliquando ad nostratium commoditatem et auxilium abscondere et sepelire decrevi: qua quidem intellect facile passunt ad lucem abscondita efferre.

> *(A table of the locations of the possessions and the hidden treasures of Menabon of Gordanig, soldier and expelled Danish chieftain; [and] of many other distinguished men in the southern part of Britain fighting against its military occupiers: which I ordered here to be hidden and buried, with the consent of those closest to me, for the benefit and advantage of those of us returning at some future time. Whereby, indeed when they have understood it [i.e. the table], they may easily bring what was hidden to light.)*[76]

The names attributed to the ten places indicated on the map are recorded by Dee as follows:

1. Gilds cros hic o ... croces mer id io onali .ot on
2. blankes Suters croces
3. Marsars got cros
4. Huteos Cros
5. Fleds grenul
6. Mons Mene
7. Mountegles arnid
8. Lan sapant

---

75. Incorrectly transliterated by Dee as 'Gordanili'. It is possible, this could be the Gordano Valley area in North Somerset. Roman coin hoards were found in Clapton-in-Gordano in 1891 and the early 1920s. [REC]   76. Translation by Barbara Prichard.

APPENDIX D

    9. Corts neld

    10. Mnrr[77] Merse

Dee indicated – in a marginal note – that the map and cipher were found by Kelley and a local man, Master John Husy, at Huteos Cross near Blockley, together with a book on magic and alchemy, having been guided there by a spirit. Dee also notes that the Danes (referred to in the cipher text) were last in England in the year 1040.

As to the treasure itself, little is known, although a book, a scroll and a powder – probably of alchemic significance – are mentioned in later sections of the diaries. Dee suggests that Kelley looks first towards Newbury in his quest, and it seems that the scryer did in fact set off in this direction in search of the treasure. Later, through the intervention of spirits, Dee was told that it was sufficient to obtain earth from the ten locations indicated in the map to bring the treasure to light. As an alternative to digging, this method seems to have been favoured by Dee and Kelley, although we have no records of their success in this matter. Whether or not the treasure or, for that matter, the monuments indicated on Kelley's map ever existed, must possibly remain a subject of conjecture.

[Nearly all the sites are still undiscovered to this day. Only one has been identified with any certainty. This is Mons Mene, now known as Meon Hill, an Iron Age hill fort in South Warwickshire on the north-eastern edge of the Cotswolds near Lower Quinton. The hill is notorious for the ritual sacrifice of agricultural worker Charles Walton on St Valentine's Day, 1945. Unlike the other places, the hill is easily traceable in the *Concise Oxford Dictionary of English Place-Names*. In 1824, a hoard of 394 iron currency bars was unearthed near the centre. Was this

77. Dee thinks this name to be Marr. [RT]

THE HEPTARCHIA MYSTICA

the treasure? Huteos or Huet's Cross, the fourth site on the map, was probably located on Northwick Hill near Blockley. Dee notes in his Diary on 23 March 1583, that the hill was where the map and the other items were found; then later, on

Meon Hill, Lower Quinton, Warwickshire. (Photograph© R.E. Cousins).

11 April, he refers to them as being discovered at Huet's Cross.

The sketch of the cross reveals that it was already severely damaged with only part of the shaft remaining. Unsurprisingly, not a fragment is traceable in the area today, but the find was undoubtedly the 'treasure' of Huteos Cross. - REC]

Like the Voynich manuscript, the end of the tale is yet untold; we can only hope that one day the final chapter will be written.

APPENDIX E
THE HEPTARCHICAL ANGELIC HIERARCHY: AN OVERVIEW
BY ROBIN E. COUSINS

With Kelley's arrival in Mortlake on 10 March 1582, the Angelic System started to develop and Dee's whole magical operations received an immediate overhaul to include the *Heptarchia Mystica* with the Holy Table, Sigillum Dei Æmeth and other magical equipment such as the Lamen and magical ring.

The *Heptarchia* was mostly transmitted during March & April 1582, but further communications in November and in April and May 1583 refined the system. The transmission of the system is recorded in Dee's spiritual diaries (*Mysteriorum Libri Quinque*) which have been published as *John Dee's Five Books of Mysteries* (San Francisco: Weiser 2003). Later Dee wrote a separate manuscript that is now part of BL Sloane MS 3191 and forms the foundation of this work.

As has been seen from the text, the *Heptarchia* is a system for harnessing the angelic forces of the seven traditional planets and the seven days of the week. The importance of seven is first emphasised in the manuscript with the opening quotation by Clement of Alexandria.

THE HEPTARCHIA MYSTICA

"The whole world is arranged in Sevens, of all that is brought to life and is born."

On 21 March 1582, the Archangel Michael expands this:

"Mark this Mystery. Seuen comprehendeth the Secrets of Heven and earth,
Seuen knitteth mans sowle and body togither. (3 in sowle, and 4 in body).
In 7, thow shalt finde the Unitie.
In 7, thow shalt finde the Trinitie
In 7, thow shalt fine the Sonne, and the proportion of the Holy Ghoste, O God, O God,
O god, Thy name (O God) be praysed euer, from thy 7 Thrones, from thy 7 Trumpets and from thy 7 Angels
In 7, God wrowght all things.
Note: In 7, and by 7 must you work all things.
O Seuen tymes Seuen, Veritie, Vertue and Maiestie." [78]

On 29 April 1582, Michael continues:

"Herein lyre theyr names that work under God upon earth: not of wicked, but of the Angels of Light. They are the Angels of the Light of our God. The Whole Gouernment doth consist in the hands of 49: (in God his Powre, Strength, Mercy, and Iustice) whose names are here euident, excellent, and glorious. Mark these Tables. Mark them. Record them to your Cumfort." [79]

The '49' or the 'Gouerment' are the 49 good angels of the planets and the days of the week. It is to them that requests are made. They are subject to the Angels of Light and their names are detailed on the circular table or planetary wheel,

---

78. John Dee's Five Books of Mysteries, p. 126. 79. Ibid., p. 166-7.

APPENDIX E

Tabula Angelorum Bonorum (See *Heptarchia*, Cap. 7). The Angels of Light consist of 4 groups. In descending order, they are as follows:

1. **DAUGHTERS OF LIGHT**
E • Me • Ese • Iana ★ Akele • Azdobn ★ Stimcul
(E is really a combined E and L, and is often written as EL)

2. **SONS OF LIGHT**
I • Ih • Ilr • Dmal • Heeoa • Beigia • Stimcul

3. **DAUGHTERS OF THE DAUGHTERS OF LIGHT**
S • Ab • Ath • Ized • Ekiei • Madimi • Esemeli

4. **SONS OF THE SONS OF LIGHT**
IL • An • Ave • Liba • Rocle • Hagonl (el) • Ilemese
(IL is really a combined E and L, as is also the "el" of Hagonel)

All these Angels of Light feature on the Sigillum Æmeth, which acts as a mandala to draw down the divine and angelic power into the crystal that stands on the seal in the centre of the Holy Table. The outside rim of the Sigillum contains various divine names. These are followed by those of the Archangels. The Angels of Light are next in the hierarchy, occupying the central hexagrams and the hexagon in their midst. The seven traditional planetary angels follow located around the pentagram within the hexagon:

ZABATHIEL	Saturn
ZEDEKIEL	Jupiter
MADIMIEL	Mars
SEMELIEL	Sun / Sol
NOGAHEL	Venus

THE HEPTARCHIA MYSTICA

CORABIEL   Mercury
LAVANAEL   Moon/Luna

Finally, the power is earthed by the equal-armed cross of the elements in the centre of the pentagram and its counterpart on the reverse side of the seal with AGLA arranged around the cross. AGLA is an acronym for Ateh Gebor Le-olahm Adonai – *Thou art mighty forever, O Lord.* (See Cap. 3 for illustration).

Many of the Angels of Light appear throughout the Diaries. The Daughters of Light & their Daughters do not feature in the rituals, but undoubtedly have an unseen influence as a result of their presence on the Sigillum Æmeth. The Heptarchical rituals involve the angels of what the Archangel Michael calls *"the lower world: The Gouernors that work and rule under God: By whome you may haue powre to work such things, as shall be to God his glorie, profit of your Cuntrie, and the knowledge of his Creatures".*

These angels of 'the lower world', to whom the magician appeals, fall into two groups.

1. THE ANGELS OF THE PLANETS

Each planet has its own King, Prince and five Principal Ministers, i.e., the Forty-Nine Good Angels (*Angelorum Bonorum*) that are detailed on the Circular table. The King and Prince for each planet are in upper case letters on the diagram. They are:

PLANET	KING	PRINCE
SUN	Bobogel	Befafes
MOON	Blvmaza	Bagenol
MARS	Babalel	Bvtmono
MERCURY	Bnaspol	Brorges
JUPITER	Bynepor	Blisdon

APPENDIX E

| VENUS | Baligon | Bornogo |
| SATURN | Bnapsen | Bralges |

These names are deployed to create the letters around the edge of the Holy Table. For the names of the five attendant ministers for each planet, see the circular diagram or the table in Appendix A, Note 24.

2. ANGELS OF THE DAYS OF THE WEEK AND THEIR MINISTERS

The kings of the planets are also the kings of the corresponding day of the week. However, this does not apply to the planetary Princes, who rule a different day of the week. In addition, each King and Prince has 42 Ministers, who rule the hours of the day concerned.

DAY	KING	PRINCE
SUNDAY	Bobogel	Bornogo
MONDAY	Blvmaza (Carmara)	Bralges (Hagonel)
TUESDAY	Babalel	Bafafes
WEDNESDAY	Bnaspol	Blisden
THURSDAY	Bynepor	Bvtmono
FRIDAY	Baligon	Bagenol
SATURDAY	Bnapsen	Brorges

The names of the Kings and Princes of the Days of the Week are used to produce the Lamen worn around the neck of the magician. The Lamen links the scryer to the crystal on the Holy Table. The Angels of the Day on the Lamen will connect with their planetary equivalents around the edge of the table ensuring spiritual progression. The divine names on the Sigillum Æmeth draw down the power to the centre of the seal, where the traditional planetary angels are inscribed around the pentagram, and on which the crystal stands. The Kings and Princes of the Planets thus meet with their planetary chiefs locking together the forces from above and below. With the attention focused on the crystal, the scryer is empowered, hoping for angelic communications and visions in the crystal or the Mind's Eye.

THE 42 MINISTERS

The King and Prince of each day are served by 42 angelic ministers to govern the hours of their day, making a total of 294 angels to cover the whole week. There are six Principal Ministers per day, each one governing the following 4 hour periods

00:00 - 04:00	12:00 - 16:00
04:00 - 08:00	16:00 - 20:00
08:00 - 12:00	20:00 - 00:00

Each Principal Minister rules the first 34 minutes of the 4 hours. To cover the rest of the 4 hour slot, a further 6 angelic ministers are created by rotating the letters of the name of each Principal Minister.

For example, the Principal Minister governing the 12 – 4 am slot on Sunday is LEENARB, who rules the first 34 minutes. Rotating the letters of his name produces 6 more angels to cover the rest of the 4 hours in intervals of 34 minutes each.

EENARBL ENARBLE NARBLEE ARBLEEN RBLEENA BLEENAR

The information relating to the ministers was delivered to Dee and Kelley on 21 March 1582 and was presented in

APPENDIX E

rectangular and circular tables which are recorded in Cap. 4 above. The Table below details all the 294 ministers for the week. No mean task, it was compiled by Dave Marsh as a ready reference source for the interested reader or practitioner, for which the authors are extremely grateful.

Note: The Principal Ministers for each day are in bold type.

THE MINISTERS FOR THE DAYS OF THE WEEK

Sunday *SoL*: llr *SoSoL*: Ave *KING*: Bobogel *PRINCE*: Bornogo

00:00	00:34	01:08	01:42	02:17	02:51	03:25
LEENARB	EENARBL	ENARBLE	NARBLEE	ARBLEEN	RBLEENA	BLEENAR
04:00	04:34	05:08	05:42	06:17	06:51	07:25
LNANAEB	NANAEBL	ANAEBLN	NAEBLNA	AEBLNAN	EBLNANA	BLNANAE
08:00	08:34	09:08	09:42	10:17	10:51	11:25
ROEMNAB	OEMNABR	EMNABRO	MNABROE	NABROEM	ABROEMN	BROEMNA
12:00	12:34	13:08	13:42	14:17	14:51	15:25
LEAORIB	EAORIBL	AORIBLE	ORIBLEA	RIBLEAO	IBLEAOR	BLEAORI
16:00	16:34	17:08	17:42	18:17	18:51	19:25
NEICIAB	EICIABN	ICIABNE	CIABNEI	IABNEIC	ABNEICI	BNEICIA
20:00	20:34	21:08	21:42	22:17	22:51	23:25
AOIDIAB	OIDIABA	IDIABAO	DIABAOI	IABAOID	ABAOIDI	BAOIDIA

THE HEPTARCHIA MYSTICA

Monday *SoL*:Stimcul *SoSoL*:llemese *KING*:Blvmaza *PRINCE*:Bralges

00:00	00:34	01:08	01:42	02:17	02:51	03:25
OESNGLE	ESNGLEO	SNGLEOE	NGLEOES	GLEOESN	LEOESNG	EOESNGL
04:00	04:34	05:08	05:42	06:17	06:51	07:25
AVZNILN	VZNILNA	ZNILNAV	NILNAVZ	ILNAVZN	LNAVZNI	NAVZNIL
08:00	08:34	09:08	09:42	10:17	10:51	11:25
YLLMAFS	LLMAFSY	LMAFSYL	MAFSYLL	AFSYLLM	FSYLLMA	SYLLMAF
12:00	12:34	13:08	13:42	14:17	14:51	15:25
NRSOGOO	RSOGOON	SOGOONR	OGOONRS	GOONRSO	OONRSOG	ONRSOGO
16:00	16:34	17:08	17:42	18:17	18:51	19:25
NRRCPRN	RRCPRNN	RCPRNNR	CPRNNRR	PRNNRRC	RNNRRCP	NNRRCPR
20:00	20:34	21:08	21:42	22:17	22:51	23:25
LABDGRE	ABDGREL	BDGRELA	DGRELAB	GRELABD	RELABDG	ELABDGR

Tuesday *SoL*: Dmal *SoSoL*: Liba *KING*: Babalel *PRINCE*: Befafes

00:00	00:34	01:08	01:42	02:17	02:51	03:25
EILOMFO	ILOMFOE	LOMFOEI	OMFOEIL	MFOEILO	FOEILOM	OEILOMF
04:00	04:34	05:08	05:42	06:17	06:51	07:25
NEOTPTA	EOTPTAN	OTPTANE	TPTANEO	PTANEOT	TANEOTP	ANEOTPT
08:00	08:34	09:08	09:42	10:17	10:51	11:25
SAGACIY	AGACIYS	GACIYSA	ACIYSAG	CIYSAGA	IYSAGAC	YSAGACI
12:00	12:34	13:08	13:42	14:17	14:51	15:25
ONEDPON	NEDPONO	EDPONON	DPONONE	PONONED	ONONEDP	NONEDPO
16:00	16:34	17:08	17:42	18:17	18:51	19:25
NOONMAN	OONMANN	ONMANNO	NMANNOO	MANNOON	ANNOONM	NNOONMA
20:00	20:34	21:08	21:42	22:17	22:51	23:25
ETEVLGL	TEVLGLE	EVLGLET	VLGLETE	LGLETEV	GLETEVL	LETEVLG

APPENDIX E

Wednesday *SoL*: Ih *SoSoL*: An *King*: BNASPOL * *Prince:* BLISDON

00:00	00:34	01:08	01:42	02:17	02:51	03:25
ELGNSEB	LGNSEBE	GNSEBEL	NSEBELG	SEBELGN	EBELGNS	BELGNSE
04:00	04:34	05:08	05:42	06:17	06:51	07:25
NLINZVB	LINZVBN	INZVBNL	NZVBNLI	ZVBNLIN	VBNLINZ	BNLINZV
08:00	08:34	09:08	09:42	10:17	10:51	11:25
SFAMLLB	FAMLLBS	AMLLBSF	MLLBSFA	LLBSFAM	LBSFAML	BSFAMLL
12:00	12:34	13:08	13:42	14:17	14:51	15:25
OOGOSRS	OGOSRSO	GOSRSOO	OSRSOOG	SRSOOGO	RSOOGOS	SOOGOSR
16:00	16:34	17:08	17:42	18:17	18:51	19:25
NRPCRRB	RPCRRBN	PCRRBNR	CRRBNRP	RRBNRPC	RBNRPCR	BNRPCRR
20:00	20:34	21:08	21:42	22:17	22:51	23:25
ERGDBAB	RGDBABE	GDBABER	DBABERG	BABERGD	ABERGDB	BERGDBA

Thursday *SoL:* Heeoa *SoSoL*: Rocle *King*: Bynapor *Prince*: Bvtmono

00:00	00:34	01:08	01:42	02:17	02:51	03:25
BBARNFL	BARNFLB	ARNFLBB	RNFLBBA	NFLBBAR	FLBBARN	LBBARNF
04:00	04:34	05:08	05:42	06:17	06:51	07:25
BBAIGAO	BAIGAOB	AIGAOBB	IGAOBBA	GAOBBAI	AOBBAIG	OBBAIGA
08:00	08:34	09:08	09:42	10:17	10:51	11:25
BBALPAE	BALPAEB	ALPAEBB	LPAEBBA	PAEBBAL	AEBBALP	EBBALPA
12:00	12:34	13:08	13:42	14:17	14:51	15:25
BBANIFG	BANIFGB	ANIFGBB	NIFGBBA	IFGBBAN	FGBBANI	GBBANIF
16:00	16:34	17:08	17:42	18:17	18:51	19:25
BBOSNIA	BOSNIAB	OSNIABB	SNIABBO	NIABBOS	IABBOSN	ABBOSNI
20:00	20:34	21:08	21:42	22:17	22:51	23:25
BBASNOD	BASNODB	ASNODBB	SNODBBA	NODBBAS	ODBBASN	DBBASNO

THE HEPTARCHIA MYSTICA

Friday *SoL*: I *SoSoL*: II *KING*: Baligon *PRINCE*: Bagenol

00:00	00:34	01:08	01:42	02:17	02:51	03:25
AOAYNNL	OAYNNLA	AYNNLAO	YNNLAOA	NNLAOAY	NLAOAYN	LAOAYNN
04:00	04:34	05:08	05:42	06:17	06:51	07:25
LBBNAAV	BBNAAVL	BNAAVLB	NAAVLBB	AAVLBBN	AVLBBNA	VLBBNAA
08:00	08:34	09:08	09:42	10:17	10:51	11:25
IOAESPM	OAESPMI	AESPMIO	ESPMIOA	SPMIOAE	PMIOAES	MIOAESP
12:00	12:34	13:08	13:42	14:17	14:51	15:25
GGLPPSA	GLPPSAG	LPPSAGG	PPSAGGL	PSAGGLP	SAGGLPP	AGGLPPS
16:00	16:34	17:08	17:42	18:17	18:51	19:25
OEEOOEZ	EEOOEZO	EOOEZOE	OOEZOEE	OEZOEEO	EZOEEOO	ZOEEOOE
20:00	20:34	21:08	21:42	22:17	22:51	23:25
NLLRLNA	LLRLNAN	LRLNANL	RLNANLL	LNANLLR	NANLLRL	ANLLRLN

Saturday *SoL*: Beigia *SoSoL*: Hagonl *KING*: Bnapsen *PRINCE*: Brorges

00:00	00:34	01:08	01:42	02:17	02:51	03:25
BANSSZE	ANSSZEB	NSSZEBA	SSZEBAN	SZEBANS	ZEBANSS	EBANSSZ
04:00	04:34	05:08	05:42	06:17	06:51	07:25
BYAPARE	YAPAREB	APAREBY	PAREBYA	AREBYAP	REBYAPA	EBYAPAR
08:00	08:34	09:08	09:42	10:17	10:51	11:25
BNAMGEN	NAMGENB	AMGENBN	MGENBNA	GENBNAM	ENBNAMG	NBNAMGE
12:00	12:34	13:08	13:42	14:17	14:51	15:25
BNVAGES	NVAGESB	VAGESBN	AGESBNV	GESBNVA	ESBNVAG	SBNVAGE
16:00	16:34	17:08	17:42	18:17	18:51	19:25
BLBOPOO	LBOPOOB	BOPOOBL	OPOOBLB	POOBLBO	OOBLBOP	OBLBOPO
20:00	20:34	21:08	21:42	22:17	22:51	23:25
BABEPEN	ABEPENB	BEPENBA	EPENBAB	PENBABE	ENBABEP	NBABEPE

APPENDIX E

It is important to establish a sacred space in which to work the ritual. The Lesser Banishing Ritual of the Pentagram is an effective way of achieving this. Choose the appropriate King and Prince for the request. Their functions can be gleaned from Caput 4 and Cap. 7 of the *Heptarchia*.

Conduct the ritual on the correct day and acknowledge the angelic ministers ruling the time slot(s) concerned. Start the operation sufficiently early to ensure the ceremony does not stray into the next day. Remember the Invocation to God (see Cap. 5) must be recited thrice daily with the last one immediately preceding the ritual.

While making the invocations the magician must stand on the relevant circular seal of the 42 Ministers overlaid with the Seal of the Prince. Hold the appropriate Seal of the King, which contains the King's name and the associated Son of the Son of Light. For further information and details of the Seals, see Cap. 3, Caput 4 and Appendices A (Notes 4 and 10) and B.

Both the King and the Prince must be invoked (see Cap. 6) with all requests being included in the invocation to the Prince. The prayer to the King invites him to appear with his Prince and his Ministers. Then, presuming they have all come, the Prince can be asked for the specific request, which is introduced via the prayer to the Prince. The text states that the *Gloria Patri* ("Glory be to the father, to the Son, and to the Holy Ghost, as it was in the beginning, is now and ever shall be, world without end, Amen") should be said after the invocation to the King; and the *Pater Noster* (the Lord's Prayer) after that to the Prince. If the Christian liturgy is felt inappropriate, just omit or employ suitable substitutes. Follow the invocations with a meditation concentrating on the nature of the request.

THE HEPTARCHIA MYSTICA

When deemed complete, close and thank all forces. Finally, perform the Lesser Banishing Ritual or chosen method of spiritual cleansing in order to purify the working space or temple.

SELECT BIBLIOGRAPHY

MANUSCRIPTS (BRITISH LIBRARY)
Sloane MS 3188. *Mysteriorum Libri Quinque* in Dee's hand.
Sloane MS 3191, Art 3. *De Heptarchia Mystica* in Dee's hand.
Sloane MS 3677. Ashmole's transcript of Sloane 3188.
Sloane MS 3678. Elias Ashmole's transcript of Sloane 3191.
Additional MS 36,674. Magical Treatises by Caius, Forman, Dee and Kelley.

PRINTED WORKS
BRUMBAUGH, Robert S. *The Solution of the Voynich Roger Bacon' Cipher.* Yale University Library Gazette, 1975.
BRUMBAUGH, Robert S. *The Voynich Roger Bacon' Cipher Manuscript: Deciphered Maps of the Stars.* Journal of the Warburg and Courtauld Institutes, Vol. 39 (1976).

BUTLER, E. M. *Ritual Magic.* Cambridge University Press, 1979.

DEACON, Richard. *John Dee.* London: Frederick Muller, 1968.

DEE, John. *A True and Faithful Relation of what passed for many Yeers Between Dr John Dee . . . and Some Spirits*, ed. by Meric Casaubon. London, 1659.
DEE, John. *John Dee's Five Books of Mystery.* San Francisco: Weiser, 2003.
DEE, John. *The Hieroglyphic Monad*, tr. J. W. Hamilton-Jones. London, 1947.
DEE, John. *The Private Diary of Dr John Dee,* ed. James O. Halliwell. London: Camden Society, 1842.

THE HEPTARCHIA MYSTICA

D'LMPERIO, M.E. *The Voynich Manuscript: An Elegant Enigma.* Fort George G. Meade, Maryland: National Security Agency / Central Security Service, 1978.

DuQUETTE, Lon Milo. *Enochian Vision Magick.* San Francisco: Weiser Books, 2008.

FRENCH, Peter J. *John Dee – The World of an Elizabethan Magus.* London: Routledge & Kegan Paul, 1972.

JAMES, Geoffrey. *Enochian Evocation of Dr John Dee.* San Francisco: Weiser, 2009.

KAHN, David. *The Codebreakers.* Sphere Books, 1977.

KRAUS, Hans P. *Thirty-five manuscripts including the St Blasien Psalter, the Llangattock Hours, the Gotha Missal, the Roger Bacon (Voynich) Cipher MS.* New York, 1962.

LAYCOCK, Donald C. *The Complete Enochian Dictionary.* York Beach, ME: Weiser, 2001.

LEITCH, Aaron. *The essential Enochian grimoire.* Woodbury, Minnesota: Llewellyn, 2014.

NEWBOLD, William R., & Roland G. Kent. *The Cipher of Roger Bacon.* Century Bookbindery, 1983.

ROWSE, A.L. *The Case Books of Simon Forman.* London: Weidenfeld & Nicolson, 1974.

SCOT, Reginald. *The Discoverie of Witchcraft.* London: Centaur Press, 1964.

SMITH, Thomas. *The Life of John Dee,* tr. William A. Ayton. London: The Theosophical Publishing Society, 1908. Originally published as *Vita Joannis Dee,* 1707.

SELECT BIBLIOGRAPHY

SUMMERS, Montague, *Witchcraft and Black Magic*. London: Rider, 1946.

TYSON, Donald. *Enochian Magick for Beginners.* St Paul: Minnesota: Llewellyn, 1997.

THE VOYNICH MANUSCRIPT, ed. by Raymond Clemens with an Introduction by Deborah Harkness. New Haven and London: Beinecke Rare Book and Manuscript Library in association with Yale University Press, 2016. A full-colour facsimile with additional essays.

WAITE, A. E.(ed.)*The Alchemical Writings of Edward Kelley.* London: Stuart & Watkins, 1970.

WAITE, A. E. *The Brotherhood of the Rosy Cross*. New York: University Books, 1961.

WAY, Peter. *Codes and Ciphers*. London: Aldus Books, 1977.

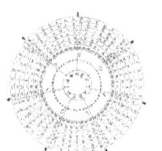

OTHER TITLES BY THOTH PUBLICATIONS

EXPLORING ENOCHIAN WORLDS
Robin E. Cousins

"Understand, therefore, that from the fire to the earth, there are 30 places or abidings: one above and beneath another."

This is the Angel Nalvage describing the Thirty Æthyrs surrounding the Four Watchtowers of the terrestrial world of the four elements to John Dee and Edward Kelley during the reception of the Enochian system of Angel Magic in 1584. There is no record of Dee or Kelley exploring these angelic worlds – a journey which can offer a path to spiritual enlightenment. Over 300 years later, Aleister Crowley was the first. He recorded his scrying of the Thirty Æthyrs in *The Vision and the Voice* (1911). Other Thelemic practitioners such as Lon Milo Duquette and David Shoemaker have subsequently published their experiences.

Now join Robin E. Cousins and friends scrying through the Watchtowers and the Æthyrs in both solo and group workings and read their visionary revelations. They preferred to employ the original system of Dee and Kelley rather than the over-elaborate revision devised by the Hermetic Order of the Golden Dawn (Neo-Enochiana) and favoured by Crowley and his followers.

To obtain ones's Enochian bearings an overview of the Angelic Universe is provided detailing the Watchtowers and the Æthyrs, plus the rituals, invocations and calls required to cross the threshold into these magical and mysterious realms.

Included are many diagrams, original and historic photographs, a detailed itinerary of Crowley's Algerian odyssey through the Æthyrs, and an exposition of the differences between the original and the Golden Dawn Enochian system.

ISBN 978-1-870450-911

SECRETS OF A GOLDEN DAWN TEMPLE
by Chic Cicero and Sandra Tabatha Cicero

A Hands on Manual for Building a Complete Golden Dawn Temple and Understanding its Symbolism.

The act of constructing a wand or other ritual object is an act of magic. The magician spends an extraordinary amount of time creating ritual objects, not because it is only through these objects that magic can rightly be performed, but because the act of creating is a magical process of growth, one which initiates the development of the will in accordance with the divine intent or purpose. This in turn contributes to the success of the ritual.

The construction of a ritual object should be treated like any other magical operation. It should focus all parts of the magician's mind (intellect, creativity, imagination, spiritual self) into one purpose – to manifest an object which will be a receptacle for higher forces, in order that the magician too can become a worthy receptacle of that which is divine.

It is not necessary to create a perfect work of art. A person who works long and hard on a wand that looks crude will ultimately have more success than a person who purchases a ready-made wand that is flawless. With this book, clear instructions are finally available on how to fabricate the wands and implements of the Golden Dawn, some of the most significant, profound and beautiful of all the ritual tools that have ever been produced in the Western Magical Tradition.

The various tools presented here each have a very specific symbology attached to them. With the materials and tools available to the modern magician, these instruments can be recreated with stunning accuracy and magnificence.

Chic Cicero and S. Tabatha Cicero have been instrumental in preserving the mystical wisdom of the Hermetic Order of the Golden Dawn. Their *Secrets of a Golden Dawn Temple: The Alchemy and Crafting of Magickal Implements* was the first book to bring you detailed instructions on crafting and using the ritual implements of the Golden Dawn system of magic. Now their classic text has been updated.

This is the most complete book to date on the construction of the many tools used in the Golden Dawn system of magic. Here is a unique compilation of the various tools of the Golden Dawn, all described in full: wands, swords, elemental tools, Enochian Tablets, altars, temple furniture, banners, pillars, thrones, lamens, mantles and robes, ritual headdresses and ceremonial clothing, admission badges, and much more. This book provides complete step-by-step instructions for the construction of nearly 80 different implements, all displayed in photographs or drawings, along with the exact symbolism behind each and every item.

ISBN 978-1-870450-64-5 400 pages

PRINCIPLES OF HERMETIC PHILOSOPHY
Dion Fortune & Gareth Knight

Principles of Hermetic Philosophy was the last known work written by Dion Fortune. It appeared in her Monthly letters to members and associates of the Society of the Inner Light between November 1942 and March 1944.

Her intention in this work is summed up in her own words: "The observations in these pages are an attempt to gather together the fragments of a forgotten wisdom and explain and expand them in the light of personal observation."

She was uniquely equipped to make highly significant personal observations in these matters as one of the leading practical occultists of her time. What is more, in these later works she feels less constrained by traditions of occult secrecy and takes an altogether more practical approach than in her earlier, well known textbooks.

Gareth Knight takes the opportunity to amplify her explanations and practical exercises with a series of full page illustrations, and provides a commentary on her work

ISBN 978-1-870450-34-8

THE STORY OF DION FORTUNE
As told to Charles Fielding and Carr Collins.

Dion Fortune and Aleister Crowley stand as the twentieth century's most influential leaders of the Western Esoteric Tradition. They were very different in their backgrounds, scholarship and style.

But, for many, Dion Fortune is the chosen exemplar of the Tradition – This book tells of her formative years and of her development.

At the end, she remains a complex and enigmatic figure, who can only be understood in the light of the system she evolved and worked to great effect.

There can be no definitive "Story of Dion Fortune". If incomplete, this retrospect provides an insight which provides understanding of her service to her times and ours. Readers may find themselves led into an experience of initiation as envisaged by this fearless and dedicated woman.

ISBN 978-1-870450-33-1

THE CIRCUIT OF FORCE
by Dion Fortune.
With commentaries by Gareth Knight.

In "The Circuit of Force", Dion Fortune describes techniques for raising the personal magnetic forces within the human aura and their control and direction in magic and in life, which she regards as 'the Lost Secrets of the Western Esoteric Tradition'.

To recover these secrets she turns to three sources.
a) the Eastern Tradition of Hatha Yoga and Tantra and their teaching on raising the "sleeping serpent power" or kundalini;

b) the circle working by means of which spiritualist seances concentrate power for the manifestation of some of their results;

c) the linking up of cosmic and earth energies by means of the structured symbol patterns of the Qabalistic Tree of Life.

Originally produced for the instruction of members of her group, this is the first time that this material has been published for the general public in volume form. Gareth Knight provides subject commentaries on various aspects of the etheric vehicle, filling in some of the practical details and implications that she left unsaid in the more secretive esoteric climate of the times in which she wrote.

Some quotes from Dion Fortune's text:

"When, in order to concentrate exclusively on God, we cut ourselves off from nature, we destroy our own roots. There must be in us a circuit between heaven and earth, not a one-way flow, draining us of all vitality. It is not enough that we draw up the Kundalini from the base of the spine; we must also draw down the divine light through the Thousand-Petalled Lotus. Equally, it is not enough for our mental health and spiritual development that we draw down the Divine Light, we must also draw up the earth forces. Only too often mental health is sacrificed to spiritual development through ignorance of, or denial of, this fact."

"....the clue to all these Mysteries is to be sought in the Tree of Life. Understand the significance of the Tree; arrange the symbols you are working with in the correct manner upon it, and all is clear and you can work out your sum. Equate the Danda with the Central Pillar, and the Lotuses with the Sephiroth and the bi-sections of the Paths thereon, and you have the necessary bilingual dictionary at your disposal – if you known how to use it."

ISBN 978-1-870450-28-7

THE WESTERN MYSTERY TRADITION
Christine Hartley

A reissue of a classic work, by a pupil of Dion Fortune, on the mythical and historical roots of Western occultism. Christine Hartley's aim was to demonstrate that we in the West, far from being dependent upon Eastern esoteric teachings, possess a rich and potent mystery tradition of our own, evoked and defined in myth, legend, folklore and song, and embodied in the legacy of Druidic culture.

More importantly, she provides practical guidelines for modern students of the ancient mysteries, 'The Western Mystery Tradition,' in Christine Hartley's view, 'is the basis of the Western religious feeling, the foundation of our spiritual life, the matrix of our religious formulae, whether we are aware of it or not. To it we owe the life and force of our spiritual life.'

ISBN 978 1 870450 24 9

A MODERN MAGICIAN'S HANDBOOK
Marian Green

This book presents the ancient arts of magic, ritual and practical occult arts as used by modern ceremonial magicians and witches in a way that everyone can master, bringing them into the Age of Aquarius. Drawing on over three decades of practical experience, Marian Green offers a simple approach to the various skills and techniques that are needed to turn an interest into a working knowledge of magic.

Each section offers explanations, guidance and practical exercises in meditation, inner journeying, preparation for ritual, the arts of divination and many more of today's esoteric practices. No student is too young or too old to benefit from the material set out for them in this book, and its simple language may help even experienced magicians and witches understand their arts in greater depth.

ISBN 978-1-870450-43-0

AN INTRODUCTION TO RITUAL MAGIC
By Dion Fortune & Gareth Knight

At the time this was something of a unique event in esoteric publishing – a new book by the legendary Dion Fortune. Especially with its teachings on the theory and practice of ritual or ceremonial magic, by one who, like the heroine of two of her other novels, was undoubtedly "a mistress of that art".

In this work Dion Fortune deals in successive chapters with Types of Mind Working; Mind Training; The Use of Ritual; Psychic Perception; Ritual Initiation; The Reality of the Subtle Planes; Focusing the Magic Mirror; Channelling the Forces; The Form of the Ceremony; and The Purpose of Magic – with appendices on Talisman Magic and Astral Forms.

Each chapter is supplemented and expanded by a companion chapter on the same subject by Gareth Knight. In Dion Fortune's day the conventions of occult secrecy prevented her from being too explicit on the practical details of magic, except in works of fiction. These veils of secrecy having now been drawn back, Gareth Knight has taken the opportunity to fill in much practical information that Dion Fortune might well have included had she been writing today.

In short, in this unique collaboration of two magical practitioners and teachers, we are presented with a valuable and up-to-date text on the practice of ritual or ceremonial magic "as it is". That is to say, as a practical, spiritual, and psychic discipline, far removed from the lurid superstition and speculation that are the hall mark of its treatment in sensational journalism and channels of popular entertainment.

ISBN 978-1-870450-31-7 Deluxe Hardback limited edition
ISBN 978-1-870450-26-3 Soft cover edition

THE GRAIL SEEKER'S COMPANION
By John Matthews & Marian Green

There have been many books about the Grail, written from many differing standpoints. Some have been practical, some purely historical, others literary, but this is the first Grail book which sets out to help the esoterically inclined seeker through the maze of symbolism, character and myth which surrounds the central point of the Grail.

In today's frantic world when many people have their material needs met some still seek spiritual fulfilment. They are drawn to explore the old philosophies and traditions, particularly that of our Western Celtic Heritage. It is here they encounter the quest for the Holy Grail, that mysterious object which will bring hope and healing to all. Some have come to recognise that they dwell in a spiritual wasteland and now search that symbol of the Grail which may be the only remedy. Here is the guide book for the modern seeker, explaining the history and pointing clearly towards the Aquarian Grail of the future. John Matthews and Marian Green have each been involved in the study of the mysteries of Britain and the Grail myth for over thirty-five years.

In *The Grail Seeker's Companion* they have provided a guidebook not just to places, but to people, stories and theories surrounding the Grail. A reference book of Grailology, including history, ritual, meditation, advice and instruction. In short, everything you are likely to need before you set out on the most important adventure of your life.

'This is the only book that points the way to the Holy Grail in the 21st century.' *Quest*

ISBN 978-1-870450-49-2

www.ingramcontent.com/pod-product-compliance
Lightning Source LLC
Chambersburg PA
CBHW040259170426
43193CB00020B/2941